It's Never Just About the Behaviour

Claire English

It's Never Just About the Behaviour

A holistic approach to classroom behaviour management

CORWIN

CORWIN
A SAGE Publishing Company

1 Oliver's Yard
55 City Road
London EC1Y 1SP

2455 Teller Road
Thousand Oaks
California 91320

Unit No 323-333, Third Floor, F-Block
International Trade Tower
Nehru Place, New Delhi – 110 019

8 Marina View Suite 43-053
Asia Square Tower 1
Singapore 018960

First published in 2024

Editor: Amy Thornton
Senior project editor: Chris Marke
Cover design: Wendy Scott
Typeset by: C&M Digitals (P) Ltd, Chennai, India
Printed and bound by CPI roup (UK) Ltd, Croydon, CR0 4YY

Library of Congress Control Number: 2023951009

British Library Cataloguing in Publication data

A catalogue record for this book is available from the British Library

ISBN 978-1-5296-2842-5
ISBN 978-1-5296-2843-2 (pbk)

Contents

Dedication

To each and every one of my students, past and present.
You are, in fact, my most influential teachers.

Acknowledgements

Navigating being a first-time mum while navigating the journey of authoring a book doesn't happen without sacrifice, sleeplessness and, certainly, the right support. That's why, when it comes to acknowledgements, I must start with the one person this book simply wouldn't exist without, my husband James. Along with quitting your job to be a stay-at-home dad, and the boundless patience and love you've shown me, your belief in my ability to write this book and still be the best mum to our little girl never faltered (even when my own self-belief did). To my sweet girl, Ava. You have grown alongside this book, completely unperturbed by my deadlines. From sending in my first drafts with all 6lbs of you snuggled safely to my chest, to putting the finishing touches on a completed manuscript with you boisterously crawling and chortling around the flat, I can only hope that despite the time and the sacrifice that this book has taken Mummy has made you as proud of her as she is of you.

Onto the book itself, which is a tapestry of the millions of micro-moments that have shaped me as a teacher: the approximate 15,600 hours spent teaching in a class-room, the hundreds of students who joined me in that space with all its trials and triumphs, the colleagues who worked alongside me, the leaders who I have learnt from, whether it be from the positive, or the negative. Although grateful for each delicate thread, I would like to give special mention to the brilliant Cara Cobden and Rachel Devlin, my first mentors who took me under their wings when I had a far fresher face and much less of a clue. Your guidance, (sometimes scarily) high expectations and the way you both 'led from the front' has become the blueprint for what I aspire to provide for other teachers.

To those whose hard work is quietly hiding in the pages of this book; to the publisher Amy Thornton: you drew a wild-card signing on a heavily-pregnant Claire, knowing that there would be competing priorities (and potentially missed deadlines) at play. You believed in me and, in doing so, gave me the opportunity to support teachers in ways I never thought possible. To the editor, Ruth Lilly: along with the obvious job of making my work far more readable, you instilled in me the confidence to push through crippling imposter syndrome and continue to dump words (the good and the bad) onto the page. To the illustrator, Suzie Hacker: your brilliant and creative mind injected life into whatever idea I threw your way, no matter how disjointed or unimaginatively communicated. To Amy Galea, my beautiful friend and incredible teacher: not only am I grateful for how much time you invested in lovingly combing through these pages, but your words, 'This book is so important', carried me through some incredibly challenging days. Thank you.

Finally, you. My fellow teacher. By picking up this book you are allowing me to weave new threads into the tapestry that makes up *you* and *your practice*. That takes trust and vulnerability. Being able to support you, to support your students, is a true privilege.

About the Author

Claire English is an experienced Australian secondary English teacher and senior leader specialising in supporting students with complex social, emotional and mental health needs. Over her career, she has worked across the United Kingdom and Australia, dedicated to transforming volatile, challenging and chaotic learning environments into places of safety, support and learning. With an unwavering belief that in order to champion all students, you must first champion all teachers, Claire founded The Unteachables Academy, where teachers are able to access relevant and actionable support through her online training, community and podcast.

Introduction

20 minutes

That is the total amount of time I was explicitly taught about classroom management over two degrees and five years.

'When students aren't listening, or doing what you've asked, you've got a few options,' my tutor proclaimed. He stood front and centre, pulled his glasses halfway down his nose and dramatically shot us his sternest 'teacher look' before breaking out of character and into a chortle.

'Then if they *still* aren't following instructions' … He raced to where we were sitting, paused for a moment and delivered a dozen rapid taps to the open page of the book in front of us, 'this'll get them back on track.' He then walked around the room, demonstrating the 'how tos' of squashing disruptive and undesirable behaviour: a finger point here, an attention-grabbing throat clear there.

A studious few wrote notes, others awkwardly commented among themselves and some were trying their darndest to avoid eye contact. I was dismayed. I was yet to step into a classroom and, although I didn't know what was awaiting me on the other side, I knew I would need far more help than that.

I just didn't know how much more.

Sink, and sink some more

Surprise, surprise, the 20 minutes didn't suffice. That first day flying solo? A baptism of fire.

I was plonked in a cramped computer room located in one of the less trodden and very isolated corners of the school. A sticky note of scribbled instructions sat on the hefty pile of comprehension worksheets:

Year 8 Tech – Period 2

- Students to complete worksheets.
- Collect at the end of the lesson with names.
- Seating plan is laminated in the folder on the desk.
- Computer-free lesson.

With the class roll, worksheets and seating plan in front of me, I anxiously awaited the ringing of the bell. Then my career was off with a monumental (and quite literal) bang.

Those names on a roll? Well, they were just that, faceless names. It was 30 on one, and with no way of knowing who they were, or who to report back on, the seating plan was as useless and powerless as I was.

I was busy in my attempts to settle a large group that had amassed in the corner, headphones hanging out of ears, raucously chatting, shoving and laughing, when one jumped up on the surrounding computer tables, kicking keyboards into the class one by one. I raced over, screamed at him to get down and he looked me dead in the eye and sent a monitor crashing to the ground.

Naively, one of my biggest fears going into that lesson was that they wouldn't complete the set work for me. The reality was far worse. I couldn't keep them safe.

It was abundantly clear that nothing prepared me for the true challenges of teaching. It seemed if I was to stay the course in the profession I had one option. Cut my teeth. Get on with it. Sink or swim.

I needed to learn how to swim. Fast.

Learning to swim

I never imagined that I would be a teacher who nagged, threatened, shouted and sent students out. Yet that's exactly who I became. When teachers are bobbing around in a sea of demoralising behaviours with no life jacket on, there's very little option but to fall back on 'inherited' classroom management strategies. These punitive strategies are subconsciously passed down from our own experiences of discipline and, with nothing else to try, they simply become our ineffective and disempowering default.

Although I spent a lot of time in the beginning treading water and 'not smiling until Easter', I was one of the lucky ones. I was surrounded by incredible mentors, had access to quality professional learning and worked with immensely experienced colleagues who modelled and shared best practice daily. However, this level of support shouldn't be a stroke of luck.

Let's face it, even if every single teacher *did* receive oodles of quality on-the-job support, why should it be a teaching rite of passage to get chucked in at the deep end to 'sink or swim'? Why is there such a cavernous space to fill between what we are taught during our teaching training and the skills needed to do the job effectively?

As my years in the classroom ticked on, my 'why' didn't change, but one thing became more and more apparent. If we want to champion every student, we have to invest more into training, supporting and preparing teachers – both before they get into the classroom and when they are thrust into it.

It's Never Just About the Behaviour exists for this very purpose. It is a bridge between the theory and the practical, a mentor and a guide, a way to approach behaviour that empowers everyone in your classroom.

There is a misconception that trauma-informed and restorative approaches to behaviour are weak, airy-fairy and don't teach 'badly behaved' kids the lessons they need to learn. Friends, it is the total opposite.

When I say that this approach to classroom management empowers everyone in your classroom, the person that it empowers most of all is you.

Classroom management: A holistic approach

Before I crack into the meaty part of the book, let's just address one big question …

Who am *I* to be teaching *you*?

I haven't (yet) led entire schools, worked at a departmental level, or obtained a PhD in behavioural science.

I am loudly and proudly … a fellow teacher. That is why this book (although absolutely backed by research) is driven by my lived classroom experience and the tried-and-true strategies that I use as a part of my everyday practice.

Do I have all the answers? Oh, hell no, and anybody who claims to is misleading you. That is because behaviour, by nature, is so nuanced, so complex, so contextual, that it is impossible to approach it as if it were a simple equation.

Classroom management is never just one thing, and it's not always about the behaviour itself. Too often our approach to behaviour attempts to hold back a torrent of water at the floodgates when, instead, we need to be gently redirecting the trickling streams that lead there.

Because classroom management is something that we are 'doing' and 'living'. We walk it and we talk it through every single choice we make, whether we are sitting around planning a lesson or having a tender moment with our coffee before the school day begins. It is for this very reason that teachers need far more than a toolbox of reactive 'how tos'; instead, they should be equipped with a way of 'being' that permeates every facet of their practice.

The Seven Pillars that underpin the concepts and strategies in this book are just that. A values system and way of 'being' that anchors the 'what to do' with 'why I am doing this?'.

The Seven Pillars of holistic classroom management

Pillar 1: Be Curious

Pillar 2: Be Calm

Pillar 3: Be Compassionate

Pillar 4: Be Consistent

Pillar 5: Be Clear

Pillar 6: Be Challenging

Pillar 7: Be Connected

Within each of these pillars you will find tangible, immediate and relevant action to revolutionise your practice. The teaching world is already saturated with professional learning that leaves you thinking, 'Okay great, but tell me what I need to actually *do!*'

Through reflective questions, strategy toolboxes, step-by-step roadmaps and plenty of real-world application, this book will give you what you need to both know and do to nail classroom management, *without* sacrificing your 'why'.

Your classroom, your island

Yes, there are immense challenges within the education system, and even your unique school context, that are out of your realm of control. Yet this book is about you.

It exists to empower you to take the action that you *can* take when you walk in through your classroom door; for you to feel supported, confident and equipped to turn your own space into an island of safety and support for each one of your students.

I want you to feel ready to lead with *curiosity, connection* and *compassion*. I want your students to know that when they enter your room they will be met with the *consistency, clarity* and *challenge* needed to feel safe and to learn. I want you to feel confident that when challenging behaviours inevitably pop up, you'll be able to respond to them effectively and *calmly*. I want you to be able to do the job that you got into the profession to do, and do it damn well. Teach.

What an honour it is to meet you here in the pages of this book. To walk alongside you in your practice as you bring about great change for not only the hardest to reach and hardest to teach students, but every single student that has the privilege of being taught by you.

PILLAR 1
Be Curious

All (yes, all) behaviour has a purpose. Even the most tiresome, challenging and seemingly 'unpalatable'. Getting curious around what this purpose might be is a crucial stepping stone to not only addressing classroom behaviour but also mitigating and resolving it.

The 'bully'

Teachers, there are three words that will likely come to mind when I describe the following student: volatile, violent and unpredictable.

After all, the way Chris behaved *was* volatile, violent and unpredictable.

Chris was enrolled smack bang in the middle of an already challenging school year, marked by an increase in staff assaults, student fights and high-level disruption that buzzed through the corridors. It was unsurprising that when the principal called a morning muster and introduced him, reading an endless rap sheet from previous placements, the faces of teachers around the room screamed, 'Oh boy, here we go'.

That rap sheet? Well, he lived up to it. He presented as a textbook 'bully'. He'd walk by unsuspecting peers, giving them a whopping blow to the arm, a shove into the wall, a little trip up, or an extra hard slap to the back that would be delivered with an audible 'thud'. His demeanour would then change as he burst into raucous laughter, put his arm around the victim of his attacks and expected them to be just as jolly and jovial as he was.

But, of course, this wasn't the case.

Some students would go along with it and placate our concerns. 'Miss, chill – he was only joking.' A thinly veiled attempt at keeping their heads low and the target off their backs.

Others, of course, wouldn't have any of it. They would chase him out and around the building, corner him up and give him a week's worth of his own medicine in a single dose. You'd think that, surely, he would expect this to happen. Yet every time there was any retaliation from his peers, we would find a distraught Chris knocking on the staffroom door, sobbing as he nursed his injuries, feeling very sorry for himself indeed.

He might have *seemed* like the bravest boy in school, but he certainly wasn't the biggest or strongest. So, while he was in the business of making school a more miserable and unsafe place for other students, he was also making it pretty unsafe and miserable for himself.

The consensus from staff was clear. Somebody was going to get seriously hurt. Chris shouldn't be around other students. This school is not the place for him.

How in the world do you begin to understand, let alone break, such a complex, unsafe and seemingly random cycle? Well, we needed to know what in the world was going on for Chris, for him to lash out over and over again, yet remain shocked and surprised by the blow back. We dug about, met with his parents. We looked at his plans. We came up empty handed.

We talked to Chris, openly and honestly. We asked him questions that maybe nobody had ever asked before. Luckily for him, and for us, we struck gold.

Was he wanting to hurt other students? No.

Was he wanting to be 'alpha'? No.

Was he wanting to play the victim? Did he want attention? Was he looking to be rescued? No, no and also no.

Believe it or not, he was … *trying to make a friend.*

He had been out of education for some time and since starting at the school he had been watching on as the boys in his year group boisterously play fought. He wanted in on the friendship action and viewed these interactions as a natural and socially acceptable way to do so. This resulted in him saying hello with a blow, a shove, an insult, a slap, followed by a laugh, an arm around the shoulder, as if to say, 'Does this make us friends now?' When that invitation was (naturally) declined, it was met with disappointment and despair. In his eyes, he was opening up the door for connection, and other students were slamming it shut in his face.

Of course, this did not excuse the behaviour; it did not lessen the impact for the other students who were on the receiving end of that behaviour; it did not in any way make it okay. But what it did do was provide a golden opportunity for us to understand Chris, to teach him, to give him the skills and support he needed to make a change. And maybe, just maybe, even make a friend.

When we can get curious and begin to understand the *why* behind the behaviour, then our work can truly begin to know *what* to do. Without this why, the what becomes reactive and disconnected, leaving teachers taking stabs in the dark with strategies that are ineffective at best, escalating and damaging at worst.

It's not 'us' and 'them'

Whether we are students or teachers, we need to remember that we are simultaneously navigating the ups and downs of this life together. It's very easy to forget that, just like our students, we are baggage-laden and messy. A bunch of perfectly imperfect human beings.

As imperfect adults, we still have times where we engage in conflict, act irrationally, get upset and frustrated with others. We might shout, swear, vent, slam a door, storm out, punch a wall, say the wrong things and hurt people we care about. Some days we can do no more than give the only 30 per cent we've got. Days marked by fatigue, lethargy, or even apathy. Other days we are on top of our game, tap into that creative genius, make waves. Both days, we are doing our damn best.

Yet, somehow, traditional classroom behaviour management holds students to a higher standard of being human, despite them being less experienced in this venture and less biologically able to regulate. It doesn't take into account the sheer level of nuance involved in just being an acting, feeling, human being. We are quick to label them as lazy, as defiant, as rude, when they display all of those same human behaviours as we do. Behaviours that are us giving what we can, in the best way we can. When we have a big wobble, we expect compassion, forgiveness, acceptance and love. Younger humans should expect the same.

That is what this pillar is all about. How we, human beings, not just students, are driven by our needs and our desires. How we are biologically wired to survive in this world. And how, as a result, we aren't always going to be behaving in ways that are 'classroom appropriate'.

Not only will this pillar help you to better understand your students and their behaviour, it will also inspire a deep reflection on your own.

After all, it's about being human.

We are all just trying to meet our own needs

Nobody behaves for behaviour's sake. There is no action that is without purpose, a goal, some kind of driving force.

The purpose behind a lot of behaviours is obvious and wouldn't be given a second thought. I get up and make a cup of tea because I want a nice warm drink to help me feel relaxed. I get up to go to the toilet because I am physiologically driven to empty my bladder. I turn on the TV because I need a little entertainment.

The driving force becomes a little less obvious when it comes to the challenging behaviours that we see presenting in our classrooms. There's rarely a very clear cut and definable purpose behind a student being chronically disengaged, ripping up their work every day, or for your cheery good morning getting a big 'f**k off, miss' in return.

Even if you sat down and straight up asked them, 'Why are you behaving like this?', it's highly unlikely they would be able to explain it. Alas, there is a reason, even multiple reasons, lurking beneath each of these challenging behaviours.

The saying 'Maslow before Blooms' is becoming increasingly popular to describe how a child must meet their need for safety and belonging before advancing to that higher cognitive level in the pyramid required for learning. However, it is not quite as straightforward as Maslow's Hierarchy of Needs suggests. We don't tick off our need for safety and then jump into an elevator to continue on to love and belonging. Then once we feel as though we belong, we don't necessarily level up to learn and feel accomplished. Rather, it is less of a hierarchy that we move through in a 'unidirectional manner' and more of a continual process of satiation that we 'move back and forth between' (McLoud, 2007).

This is best explained through William Glasser's Choice Theory concept of the 'Five Basic Needs'. These needs are universal and innate, a predictable part of our shared human experience. They include:

1. the need for survival
2. the need for love and belonging
3. the need for fun
4. the need for power and mastery
5. the need for freedom.

We are constantly behaving to meet these needs, or 'fill our cups', moment to moment. When one of our cups is running a little low, that internal motivation to get

Image 1.1   What fills your cups?

up and *do something* kicks in. Even if this behaviour is less than desirable, according to Glasser (n.d.) it is still the 'best attempt to get what you want, at that point in time with the information available to you'.

Although meeting needs is a universal experience, our cups still differ in size, in style, in shape to the person next to us. Some may have a little hole in the bottom making it harder to keep full, and some might have the capacity of a thimble. This is called our 'needs profile' and is determined by all of the factors that make us unique and individual humans: our upbringing, our culture, our experiences, our personality and the stage of life we are in.

To consider our own needs profiles, we can dig a little deeper into the things that are quite often sticking points for us, things that we may focus more or less on, things that might cause friction or conflict in our lives if we don't get that need met.

Wanting to get curious about your own needs profile? Consider your behaviours during the COVID lockdowns, a time that stripped away most of the things we would usually do to keep our cups full. During the most momentous upheaval of our lifetime, what did you gravitate towards doing to make your feet feel like they were on solid ground?

Were you nurturing a stinky bubbling sourdough starter to feel a sense of mastery, or were you happier doing a pub quiz online to emulate some sense of community and fun?

Did it enrage you to see some breaking the rules, or were you driven to break the rules yourself and have a cheeky cross-bubble contamination?

Were you scoffing at the panic buyers, or piling the bog roll and tinned beans into your trolley?

Were you despairing over your lost holidays and birthday celebrations and wedding cancellations, or were you too concerned about you and your loved ones to have those things even factor in?

All these pandemic behaviours can be associated with us trying to get back in the driving seat, back in control and satiate our needs in the best way we could, given what we had at our disposal. In a (semi) post-pandemic world, our needs profile remains the same. What did it reveal about yours?

Needs-meeting in the classroom

If all behaviour has a purpose, and that purpose is to satiate a need, then the behaviours that we see playing out in our classrooms are all needs-meeting by nature. Very often, however, it is much more multifaceted than just being able to say, 'Oh, you're trying to meet your need for love and belonging!' There are endless amounts of nuance and, as you will see when I talk about the brain behind the behaviour later in this chapter, it's rarely just one thing.

But don't despair and think, 'There is absolutely no way I am ever going to be able to know what is going on!'

This chapter is less about you being able to know the exact driving force behind the behaviour, and more about you having the knowledge you need to simply get curious, see the bigger picture and consider what *may* be lurking beneath. The curiosity itself is the intervention (luckily for us because the student probably doesn't know the exact 'why' either).

Needs-meeting in our classroom is everywhere.

You only have to look as far as the phones glued to our students' hands, or the way they chat and chuckle with each other to see them trying to constantly satiate their need for *love and belonging*, *fun* and *freedom* (as I said, it's rarely one thing).

Then there are others who are in the midst of a perpetual and gallant battle for survival and *safety*. They might be in and out of the classroom, up and down from their seats, ripping their work into pieces, or pushing it off the table.

Let's not forget about that student I spoke about at the start. Without us really getting to the bottom of it, it would be easy to assume he was meeting his need for power and survival: that he was trying to position himself as a bit of a tough 'top dog' in a new and anxiety-inducing environment – when, in reality, it was love and belonging calling the shots.

Image 1.2   Filling cups in the classroom

You can't teach to a class of empty cups, but what in the world can we do about that as teachers? There are 30 kids in a room. All with different needs profiles. All with different contexts and personalities. It feels pretty impossible, but we *can* set our classrooms up to be more 'needs-meeting' by nature!

Don't worry if the following examples don't make sense to you just yet, you have a whole book to follow that is full of proactive needs-meeting teaching practice!

Of course, we can't completely eliminate challenging student behaviour. We can't even proclaim to be able to eliminate our own challenging behaviour – and that we *do* have control over! But what we can do is put the right measures in place to make students feel safe, make them feel like they belong, make them feel like they can achieve, and make them feel like they have choice. When we do these things, we start to get those cogs of proactive classroom management moving.

When needs collide

Teachers, *your* needs don't just get put on hold because you are there doing a job.

I could talk about our need for love and belonging. How our reserves are rapidly depleted when a student hits us with deeply hurtful and personal comments.

I could talk about our need for safety. How our entire body reverberates with adrenaline long after a student kicks through the door, screams at the top of their lungs, or chucks a table across the room.

But I want to talk about mastery. Because when the end of the year comes, what are teachers measured against? What is a marker of their success?

Data

Names on a page with starting points and end points. Pass. Fail. Satisfactory. Unsatisfactory. No mention of the nuances, the shades of grey, the tireless work that has gone into trying to engage a young person with complex needs and behaviours that challenge. Then what happens? A teacher's desperation to successfully deliver an often over-subscribed curriculum creates a perfect storm, driving more frustrated and punitive strategies to dealing with the behaviour that stands in their way. Strategies which inadvertently work in direct conflict with the needs of their students, escalating behaviours, fracturing relationships.

This is where holistic classroom management comes in: to run our rooms in a way that fosters love and belonging, create a cocoon of safety and security, and pave the way for learning and mastery – an environment that meets the needs of both teachers and students alike.

Stop and ponder

Next time you feel that pressure rising, next time you feel that things in the classroom aren't going the way that you had hoped, just stop for a moment and think ...

What needs am I trying to meet, right now, at this moment?

What needs do I think my students are trying to meet, right now, at this moment?

How can I, as the adult in the room, understand this and reduce the opportunity for conflict?

The brain behind the behaviour

Have you ever said, 'You know better than to do that' to one of your students?

What if I told you that even if adolescents do *technically* know better, their brains aren't quite ready to follow the same rules.

If you teach teenage students, it can be really easy to slip into a pattern of expecting them to act like little adults. After all, they are on their way to driving, working and having romantic relationships.

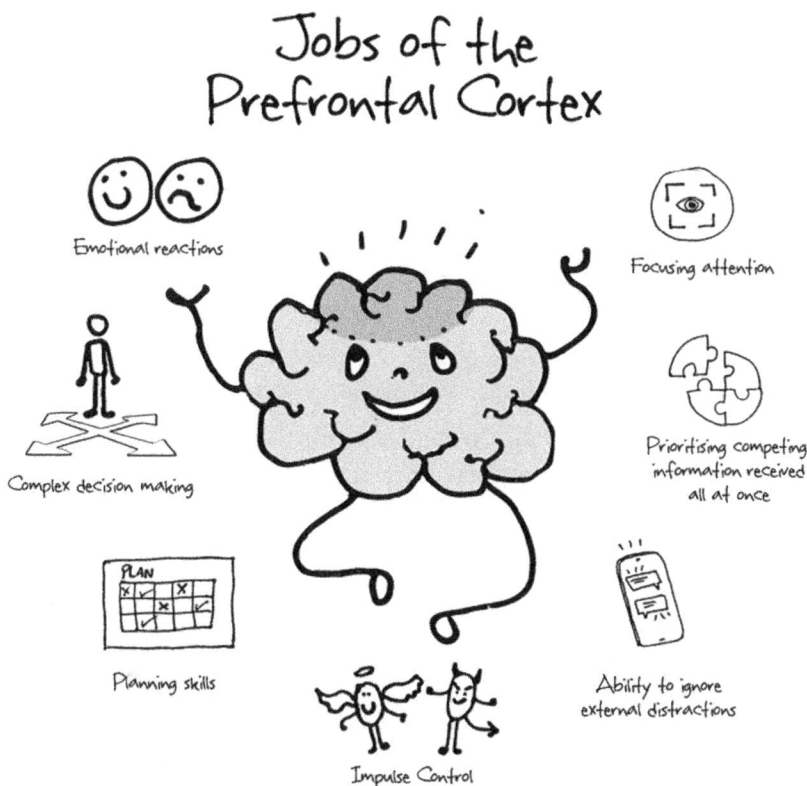

Image 1.3   Important jobs of the prefrontal cortex

However, when it comes to neurological development, their brains are still a while off finishing the job. Research shows that our brains continue to rewire and develop from puberty up until 25 years old, and the part that is rewiring itself the most is the prefrontal cortex (Arain et al., 2013). Often referred to as the 'thinking' brain, this part is responsible for all our rational, complex thought and decision making, meaning our students are still very much learning how to *think* before they *act*.

This late maturation of the 'thinking' part of the brain means that the amygdala, the 'feeling' part of the brain, calls more of the shots. As the amygdala is responsible for the immediate or 'gut' reactions (Stiles and Jernigan, 2010), you can begin to see how brain development might have a lot to answer for when it comes to *how* students are attempting to meet their needs ... with more heart, action, impulsivity and a little (or a lot) less thought.

This doesn't mean that we lower our expectations of them; on the contrary, it makes expectations even more important. Understanding their growing brains is just a tool to help us reframe behaviour as something that is less about straight up defiance and more to do with their biology.

The brain and trauma

All of those regular old biological challenges are further compounded when you mix in adverse childhood experiences and trauma.

As a teacher, it's statistically likely that this relates to at least a few of your students. In a 2014 study it was found that nine per cent of the UK population had experienced at least four adverse childhood experiences (Bellis et al., 2014), which can be defined as 'highly stressful, and potentially traumatic, events or situations that occur during childhood and/or adolescence' (Young Minds, n.d.)

Remember that the brain is under construction until an adolescent reaches their mid-20s. Until then, it is developing and pruning different connections, including creating the crucial interconnectedness between the prefrontal cortex and the amygdala (Liu et al., 2020). These two parts of the brain are designed to work together in perfect synchronicity. When the amygdala signals that a threat is about, the prefrontal cortex can calm it all down by showing the amygdala that it was either a false alarm, or that the threat has now gone away. Cue de-escalation and regulation.

However, when a child is exposed to trauma, their brains are shaped to accommodate this. It forces it to grow and adapt in ways that will help them survive and stay safe; it is both their superpower and their kryptonite. In fact, when a child is exposed to adversity and trauma, the amygdala increases in volume (Klaming et al., 2019), turning the brain into a hyper-vigilant, quicker responding, survival powerhouse. As well as making the amygdala itself more of a force to be reckoned with, some of those crucial connections between the prefrontal cortex and the amygdala are pruned away. With all of that surviving to do, there's no point trying to keep those pathways for complex decision making! This leads to a cleverly crafted hyper-reactive brain that sends its human into a more frequent state of fight or flight, and makes it far harder to find a clear road back to calm and regulation (Liu et al., 2020).

What fight, flight and freeze looks like in the classroom

A lot of the more challenging behaviours that you will come up against in the class-room could be the brain just trying to get them back to a place of safety in the best way it can.

If a student is in survival mode, it could manifest in the behaviours shown in Image 1.4.

Image 1.4   Fight, flight or freeze in the classroom

When students are in this fight, flight or freeze state, what do you think the *worst* thing we could do as their teacher might be?

The traditional response to these behaviours, such as threatening punishment, raising our voice, writing names on the board and sending them out of the room will further escalate behaviour by spiralling them deeper and faster into dysregulation.

But now that you are armed with a bit of foundational knowledge around the brain, you will be able to see these really challenging behaviours as an alarm bell signalling that things aren't quite right. You will be able to get curious, rather than furious. You will be able to be strategic, rather than reactive. It's not just about being able to approach the behaviour differently, either. Getting curious about those big behaviours that are playing out in front of us keeps our own prefrontal cortex engaged and our amygdala chilled.

Curiosity is not just about helping our students; it's about helping us. The two are as interconnected as the prefrontal cortex and the amygdala.

Curiosity in action

Have you ever been told to 'not take the behaviour personally'? If the answer is yes, you're not alone. I have been given this advice, I have given this advice and ... I hate this advice. Not because it isn't true, but because it is often said without being paired with the necessary skills or support to depersonalise it. Even if we know rationally that the behaviour isn't about us, it can still cause our own amygdala to signal that danger is afoot.

This is one of the biggest personal and professional benefits of having a little bit of an understanding about the driving forces behind the behaviour. Having this awareness supports you to keep your prefrontal cortex nice and connected. When we are in our thinking brain, we have the best chance of remaining regulated, rational, calm and curious.

Just to throw another spanner in the works before we move on, there are times when you should get a little self-reflective. We aren't perfect. When we are stressed, we can say silly things, make mistakes, get snappy. We have biases and make assumptions. We do things as teachers all the time where an apology wouldn't go astray. See these moments as powerful opportunities to model the skills of taking accountability and making amends. Remember, we are all just humans doing the best we can; our students need to see this too.

Being a behaviour detective

Remember that you may never really, truly know the cause of the behaviour, nor does this matter too much. But curiosity in itself will give you the best chance at effectively approaching and addressing behaviour in a way that connects and de-escalates. When we reflect rather than react, it emphatically says 'I care about you as a human being', something that some of your most vulnerable students might hear very little of.

So how to get curious?

Just by learning a bit about the brain and the needs driving behaviour, you are more than halfway there. The below process offers you a line of questioning by which to put this curiosity into action and hardwire it as an everyday part of your practice.

1. Observe the details of the behaviour:
    *   what behaviours are you seeing play out?
    *   are these common for the young person?
    *   are they happening at certain times of the day or particular parts of the lesson?
    *   what happened before the behaviour?

2. Use your intuition and senses:
    *   what feelings do you think are involved; are they in fight, flight or freeze?
    *   are they frustrated and bored; confused; angry; upset; embarrassed?
    *   are they unaware of what they are doing because of a lack of skill?

3. What can you deduce:
    *   what do you think they are trying to communicate?
    *   what need might they be trying to meet?
    *   what is the behaviour signalling to you?

4. Based on your findings, think about the following:
    *   how could I accommodate this need at this moment?
    *   how can I bring this student back into a regulated state?
    *   how can I pre-emptively provide support for this next time?
    *   what needs to be done to follow up on and resolve this situation?

Detective work in action

Below are a few common classroom scenarios to show you what curiosity might look like.

Scenario 1: A student won't put their phone away

1. **Observe the details:** You ask a student to put their phone away and get on with their work. They flat out refuse, looking as if they are escalating.
2. **Use your intuition:** You can see they are getting increasingly angry at you being near them. You can see they are anxious at the thought of putting their phone away.
3. **What can you deduce?** If they are anxious at the thought of putting their phone away, it could be a *flight* response. Something may have happened outside the lesson, or they might be avoiding the work.
4. **Based on your findings, what to do?** As you are not sure what it could be, and this is not common behaviour, you investigate further by engaging in a discussion with the student after the lesson. You ask them if they are okay and find out what is going on and make a plan for the next lesson (responsible phone use and a regulation strategy if necessary).

Scenario 2: Work completion

1. **Observe the details:** You get to the end of the task and you notice that a student has doodled all over the page rather than completing their work.
2. **Use your intuition:** You can tell by knowing their ability level that they might have been a bit confused by what they needed to do and possibly felt embarrassed to try.
3. **What can you deduce?** They don't feel comfortable or properly supported to complete their work for the lesson. They are choosing to sit there and doodle because they are too embarrassed to tell you.
4. **Based on your findings, what to do?** They require additional support with the task. You identify that in the following lesson you will touch base with them throughout and make them feel supported, as well as provide a scaffold for their writing with a couple of sentence starters to get them going. You check in with them about this, 'I can see you had a bit of trouble with the work today, are you okay? I plan to do XYZ next lesson.'

Scenario 3: Student interruption

1. **Observe the details:** A student keeps interrupting you while you are trying to teach.
2. **Use your intuition:** They might not understand the expectations of whole-class discussions; they don't seem to be doing it to be challenging or provocative in any way.
3. **What can you deduce?** They are doing the best they can to involve themselves in the lesson, however, they don't have the skills to do so in a way that is appropriate.
4. **Based on your findings, what to do?** Create a visual to put up on the board that acts as a reminder to put hands up and wait during whole-class discussions. Discuss this with the child and explain what this means to them and why we do this. During the lessons to follow, practice using this visual with this student and the whole class (pausing and pointing when somebody yells out during discussions).

Remember, behaviours are an expected and normal part of being human. Which brings us on to our first golden rule of holistic classroom management:

Behaviour talks, you just need to know how to listen.

Even just the act of tuning in and trying to listen can be an immediate game changer.

Curiosity about our own responses to behaviour

It's not just the students' behaviour we need to get curious about. Looking inward and getting curious about our *own* responses helps us to engage our own thinking brain and de-escalate our own stress response. As a teacher, this is key. We can't possibly address a dysregulated child if we aren't regulated ourselves – but much more on that in the next chapter.

Whether we like to hear it or not, we can very easily drive a student further into fight, flight or freeze mode. We can very easily make a situation far worse. Why? Because we are humans, of course. This isn't something that comes naturally for us; why should it? Which is why it needs to be explicitly taught and practised.

Looking inward at our own needs, our own feelings, our own stress responses and our own behaviours is a great step to making sure we can address our students in a way that will be a win–win. Sometimes reflecting on the following is the most productive thing we can do when facing the immense challenges of classroom management.

Stop and ponder

Six questions to inspire curiosity around our own responses to student behaviour:

1. What are my own needs right now? Are they being met? Is this impacting my work? What is driving my own behaviour right now?
2. Are my feeling and thinking brains connected? If not, what can I do to make sure they are?
3. Am I feeling regulated, calm and balanced?
4. What is my body telling me? Am I breathing calmly and deeply, or shallowly? Are my shoulders tight and is my jaw clenched, or are things relaxed?
5. Am I managing behaviours with my emotional downstairs brain, or my thinking upstairs brain?
6. When that student behaved in that way and I responded, what was happening for me?

Pillar 1 at a glance

- **We have Five Basic Needs.** We are all just constantly trying to satiate and 'top up' our basic needs of survival, love and belonging, fun, power and mastery and freedom. We do this through our behaviours, and each of us meet these needs in a different way.
- **These Five Basic Needs can cause conflict.** When our students' needs aren't met, or if they clash with our needs, this may result in conflict and challenging behaviour.
- **The brain isn't fully developed until 25 years of age.** This means our students are driven more heavily by the emotional, feeling part of the brain, the amygdala. The rational, thinking part of the brain, the prefrontal cortex, develops last. This has big implications for how our students behave and learn.
- **Trauma shapes the brain to be more efficient with survival.** This makes some students hyper-sensitive to triggers, resulting in more fight, flight or freeze behaviours presenting in the classroom.

- **Getting curious about a student's behaviour is a crucial first step.** Not only when it comes to supporting our most vulnerable students with complex needs, but also supporting us in depersonalising behaviour, regulating our own nervous systems and responding more effectively in the midst of tough behaviours.

Digging deeper

Listen in:

Hear me talk more about the Five Basic Needs on Episode 31 of The Unteachables Podcast: *The 'Why' That Drives Our Behaviour (The 'Good', the 'Bad' and the 'Ugly'): The 5 Basic Needs.*

Add to your bookshelf:

The Power of Showing Up: How Parental Presence Shapes Who Our Kids Becomes and How Their Brains Get Wired, Daniel J. Siegel and Tina Payne Bryson (London: Scribe, 2020).

The Whole Brain Child: 12 Proven Strategies to Nurture Your Child's Developing Mind, Daniel J. Siegel and Tina Payne Bryson (London: Robinson, 2012).

PILLAR 2
Be Calm

One of the most impactful tools we have in our classroom management arsenal is probably one of the most challenging. Embodying a sense of still and calm in a room completely incongruous to that.

Playing a game of whack-a-mole

My 'teaching wardrobe' was exclusively black. Not because I wouldn't have loved to wear something bright and bubbly, but because it would have exposed the back, chest and pit sweat I was sporting as I frantically paced around my classroom. My nickname in the staffroom? 'Sweaty beast.'

I started my teaching career in the notorious hot box of Western Sydney. In the peak of summer, it would reach a ludicrously stifling who-knows-what in the tiny, unairconditioned, body-filled classrooms. Combined with the 'I have zero control over this class' anxiety, things in Room 25 were anything but 'chilled'. Including my response to the carnage that unfolded every lesson. Heated. Frantic. Reactive.

Each lesson I would draw up a big box with a double underlined heading 'lunch detention' on the whiteboard, then flap around running back and forth as I tried to extinguish spot-fires.

Image 2.1   The vicious cycle of reactive classroom management

'Right, that's it!'

Scribbling a name and another and another. Three strikes and you're out. That's one cross. Another cross. Another cross. Three crosses reached. Wait … Now what do I do?

I think back on those lessons as a giant game of whack-a-mole. You know that arcade game where little characters pop up from holes on a board, and you need to whack them down with a mallet, as they get faster and faster and more overwhelming and increasingly difficult to keep at bay?

Yep, that is exactly what reactive classroom management is like. And it's a vicious cycle.

The answer? Well, it's staring us right in the face, but it is incredibly hard to accept, grasp and embody. You see, it starts with that first step. Us.

As teachers, we can reinstate calm, or further escalate the room, just through our own emotional influence. Little did I know that I spent most lessons dousing behaviour spot-fires with petrol, helping them spread, keeping them stoked. Little did I know that if I was to nip my freneticism and frustration in the bud and be still, be calm, be controlled and just stop freaking moving, my classroom management would have been completely and utterly transformed.

Yet I didn't know then what I know now. That it is *you*, *the teacher*, that is the single most impactful classroom management resource available. Not only can you address the challenges that pop up just through your own regulation, but you can mitigate some of them entirely.

Part 1: Calmly *mitigating* challenging behaviour

Whatever you do, don't panic

Calm feels incongruous with classroom teaching, doesn't it?

Which is why me saying 'don't panic and be calm' probably feels like a big slap in the face in relation to all those times you have been on the receiving end of behaviours that feel so personal, so triggering and, oh, so disempowering.

But please don't slam the book shut just yet because what I will be talking about in Part 1 will help you tackle something that is probably your most salient classroom management battle: the dreaded 'low-level' behaviours.

These are the whack-a-mole behaviours that you can spend all lesson, every lesson, addressing, but still never *actually* address. The behaviours that are niggling enough to completely derail a lesson, but not individually obvious or serious enough to explicitly resolve.

All of those 'little things', the hundreds of nuanced 'micro moments', that combine to add up to one big disruption ...

It is the calling out, the talking over, the tapping, the funny noises, the disengagement, the coming late and leaving early, the whispers, the chatter, the laugher, the throwing things across the room and talking with friends, the blatant 'no' to your requests. You know that the list goes on and on.

Teachers who seek support for these behaviours often get a bit of a shoulder shrug; there's no easy fix, there's no rescuing, there's no one 'big talk' you can have with a class. No expectation setting will avoid it, no consequence will shift it, you can't 'positive relationship' your way out of it.

So ... therein lies a trap. One where teachers spend all lesson trying to do the job of actually teaching, but instead are stuck being spoken over, waiting for attention, being interrupted, re-explaining the task, 'whack-a-moling' all lesson, becoming increasingly dysregulated, frustrated and disheartened – resulting in the same classroom management approach I explained in the opening of the pillar, and one that I have seen in response to low-level behaviours in most classrooms I have observed in. One that was erratic, counterproductive, ineffective and, of course, the antithesis of calm.

Your golden ticket

What is the answer here? How can we break this seemingly impossible cycle?

It's (luckily) not phone calls home, meetings with parents, detentions, suspensions, strikes on the board, losing your voice screaming for quiet, sending students out, giving them a stern talking to, getting the head teacher to come and talk to the class, bad report comments, or shocking assessment results to snap them out of it ...

No, all of that might work for a minute, a lesson, or maybe even a week, but inevitably those low-level behaviours will ramp up again as the call, talk or terror fades from their minds.

The answer is you and your teaching presence. This is the golden ticket to reducing those challenging behaviours before they even arise.

But what is teacher presence, really?

Is it a glance over the glasses? A strong 'I'll wait' game?

Is it a bubbly, energetic personality? Being extroverted, funny and charismatic? Being that 'cool' and relatable teacher?

Is it the mentality of 'don't smile until the holidays'?

Is it the ability to instil fear into the hearts and minds of little humans so they don't dare step a foot out of line?

Nope. It is none of these things.

Luckily for all my fellow awkward and introverted teachers out there, a strong teaching presence is something we can strategically craft. It is something we improve over time. It is intentional, and it is skilful. A strong teaching presence is, in fact, calm, controlled, credible and, by nature, compassionate.

The conductor and the orchestra

Think of your class as an orchestra. Your students are constantly playing to the tune of their emotional state. Without a skilled conductor, they will feed off each other, playing out of time, playing off key.

As their teacher, as the adult in the room, you are the conductor. You are there, front and centre, setting the mood of the room, doing your job of keeping the class perfectly in tune.

The music? The energy and behaviour in the room.

Your baton? Your teaching presence, which is comprised of all of your non-verbal classroom management strategies.

Every single move we make (or don't make) in our classrooms is communicating something non-verbally to our students. When I say 'non-verbal strategies', I mean more than just hand signals and visuals. It is *everything* in the classroom (except for what you say, of course).

Your presence. Your energy. Where you look. Your pace. Where you stand. *How* you stand. *How* you look. Your volume. Your movements. Your posture. Your breathing. Your expressions. Your distance. Your tone. Your everything.

These strategies all work at the pre-escalation phase. Before challenging behaviours bubble up to the surface, they are already doing their job of keeping things at bay! However, the success of this approach hinges entirely on our ability to self-regulate and remain calm.

The barriers to calm

Yes, being calm is the non-negotiable foundation of your teaching presence. Yet I am sure I don't have to tell you that it is far easier said than done. Teaching, after all, is a pretty stress-inducing job. In fact, teachers struggling with their own regulation in the classroom 'makes perfect neurobiological sense' (Gobbel, 2023b).

Imagine you have just got your raucous class settled and on-task, when a student kicks through your door, undoing all that hard work. Are you feeling calm? Probably not.

We have our own stress response, and classrooms are full of day-to-day stressors. Your brain sees that student bursting through the door as a threat and goes to work to protect you by preparing your body to fight, flight, or freeze. Your feeling brain and thinking brain are no longer on talking terms, so your ability to really think rationally about your next move is impaired.

The choice theory concept of the 'perceived' and 'quality' worlds (Glasser, 1998) helps us to further understand how challenging it might be for us to stay calm in the face of classroom challenges. The perceived world is our perception of the real world around us, and our quality world is the picture we have in our heads of what we want things to be like. We are constantly comparing our perceived world and quality world. If these two are pretty well matched, our needs are met and things feel pretty good. If they are out of balance, it drives us to behave in whatever way we can to get closer to that quality world.

In this common classroom scenario, you have a quality world where all your students are beautifully engaged and ready to learn. When your perceived world is the opposite to this you are thrown off balance and all your behaviour is driven by your desire to get back to where you want to be. All those crosses on the board, yelling over the noise, saying 'Right that's it!' is just us a desperate attempt to reach that quality world.

Overcoming this barrier

No classroom management strategy will ever cancel out a dysregulated teacher; you need to approach every single strategy and roadmap in this book from a place of calm.

However, never in the history of telling people to calm down has saying 'calm down' calmed anybody down. So, before this book becomes a giant version of me saying that, here is a three-step roadmap for accomplishing self-regulation and calm amid the chaos of a classroom.

Take a pause

It is so easy when there are so many things going on to *react* rather than *act*. The difference? When we react quickly to behaviour in the moment, it is usually driven

Image 2.2   The road to being a conductor of calm

by the emotional part of our brain. Just by giving it a bit of time, a bit of pause, a bit of space, we can transform our response to behaviour from one that is reactive to one that is more proactive.

Why does this matter? When we react to behaviour in the heat of the moment, especially when we are feeling escalated and stressed ourselves, there's a much higher chance of us escalating the behaviour of our students and making things far more difficult for ourselves. The calmer and more considered our response, the more buy-in we will get from our students. We simply can't get anywhere when we are fighting fire with fire.

Take a breath

Do not underestimate the power of the breath as a key pedagogical tool for behaviour (and I don't mean biting into an onion so your students won't want you near them, although that may work too).

When we intentionally change the way we breathe in moments of stress, we slow our heart rates, reassure our amygdala that there is no threat, reduce the stress hormone cortisol and re-engage with our rational brains. Addressing behaviour with our 'thinking' brains switched on is always going to be much more effective than leading with our 'feeling' brains.

If you find that you're feeling a little stressed out and on edge before that challenging class begins, or when you see that particularly difficult student walk in, this is a good time to take a few deep breaths and re-centre yourself. This simple act has the potential to transform how you approach that first part of the lesson, or a student about their behaviour.

Get curious

In Pillar 1 I highlighted the importance of curiosity in supporting us to self-regulate and depersonalise behaviour. Now that you are armed with the knowledge of what is going on in your brain, you can use this in the battle to keep calm.

Before a potentially challenging lesson, it is not uncommon to already feel the dread dwelling in our stomachs. If we go into that lesson unchecked, the work of de-escalation that needs to be done will become an uphill battle.

When we get into the habit of checking in with ourselves and getting curious about where we are at mentally, we increase our ability to self-regulate and therefore co-regulate with our students, bettering our chances of approaching our class, and their behaviours, calmly. Better yet, if we are regulated in this way, the work of reducing low-level behaviours is already unconsciously underway. Sounds like a pretty good trade-off to me.

Tune in and ask yourself the following questions:

- Am I feeling regulated, calm and balanced?
- What is my body telling me?
- Am I breathing calmly and deeply, or shallowly?
- Are my shoulders tight and is my jaw clenched, or are things relaxed?
- Do I need to take 30 seconds before class to just breathe and regulate?
- Am I being led by my emotional brain or my thinking brain?

Your non-verbal toolbox

Once you've mastered regulation, you've pretty much got this toolbox nailed. If you approach all these things in a calm, regulated state (even if you mess up the steps a little) you're still going to have some success. But be warned, because the opposite is also true. That is because every single one of the following strategies are driven by your own regulation. They actively work to de-escalate challenging behaviour, to foster a calm environment, to proactively minimise those frustrating low-level behaviours.

When hardwired as a part of your everyday teaching pedagogy, these seemingly simple yet highly nuanced strategies will give you a bucketload of classroom management success.

How to work the room
(to have the room work for you)

Pace
How we move

Presence
How we hold
ourselves

Present
How we talk

Credible, calm, composed

Image 2.3   How to work the room (to have the room work for you)

Non-verbal tool 1: Pace

How we move around the room in a lesson physically and energetically models the expectations we have of our students.

I spent the first few years as a teacher frantically pacing around the room. Passing out worksheets, rushing over to raised hands, running back and forth between the board, the door, a desk, the laptop, that student who was ripping up their work, the board again. I had no idea that I was actually making things far more difficult for myself.

If you're wanting a calm and settled class, slow it right down.

Now if you were doing a task that required higher energy and movement, go for gold!

Match it!

Do a song and dance!

It is all about mirroring what you want from your students at that moment.

Non-verbal tool 2: Presence

How we hold ourselves, and our general *presence* makes a huge difference to how our students respond to us. Sometimes we are more relaxed and open to a bit of a chit chat, sometimes we mean business and are more credible. Both are important, we just need to know when to use them.

Think about posture. If we are leaning and relaxed, this is inviting more of a casual and chatty atmosphere with our students.

When we are standing up straight and still, we are credible and serious. This sends messages to students that we are ready for them to embody that same tone.

Non-verbal tool 3: Present

How we present verbal information to our students sends more messages than what is actually being said. We can be loud, quiet, formal, informal, bubbly, flat. We can use upwards or downwards inflections. We can speak quickly or slow it right down. All of these decisions are non-verbally communicating and modelling expectations to our students. They tell them whether they are expected to contribute or just listen, whether it is a time to seriously crack on with the work or be playful and silly, whether you're happy for them to have a chat, or you're asking for quiet work. All without any verbal instruction.

Crafting your non-verbal teaching persona

In my second year of teaching, I had the 'bottom' Year 8 class and the 'top' Year 10 class (I will be delving into why I despise these labels in the next pillar). The Year 8 class was almost entirely populated by notoriously challenging students. It was the kind of class you'd get assigned to and spend the whole of summer feeling the anxiety bubble up and over as the year grew nearer.

The Year 10 class, however, were a beautifully charming, funny and studious bunch that I could not wait to jump in with. I was excited for literary debates and interesting thesis points, and, of course, fewer issues with behaviour. After all, they were going to be really focused on their studies ... right? Right?

Well, it started out exactly how one would expect. The Year 8 class was a chaotic mix of chatter, fights, tipped over chairs and a constant game of bin basketball with empty water bottles and ripped up paper. In contrast, the Year 10 class was a much-needed respite from the havoc of the day.

Until something changed. By the end of the first term, after just 12 weeks, it had been flipped on its head. I found myself dreading those loud, arrogant and lazy Year 10s, and not minding the cheeky chatter of the Year 8s, who, most days, happily and easily just 'got on with it'.

At the time I blamed them. *They* were choosing to listen or not to listen. *They* were choosing to work or be lazy. *They* were choosing. Yet looking back, *I* now know that *I* was choosing.

Because of my preconceived ideas of the types of students in both classes, I made the mistake of treating them differently, acting differently, having different expectations, being a different conductor in both spaces. It wasn't obvious to me at the time, but I was sending powerful messages through everything I was doing pedagogically in those two classes. I simply didn't know, what I didn't know.

I would brace myself for the Year 8 class, get everything ready and take a breath before the lesson would start. I'd greet them at the door and send them in quietly so they wouldn't bounce in with elbows flailing. I would be warm and welcoming, yet posed and credible, as they found their assigned seats. I would talk softly, move slowly, step lightly, as if treading over a minefield. I would settle myself in to wait for attention, dropping my shoulders, standing straight, breathing deep into my belly. I would be consistent in communicating and holding boundaries and expectations every single lesson, not giving an inch in fear that they would take a mile. I would get to the end of the 75 minutes, happy and relieved, sending them off row by row after they had cleaned up around their desks with a hi-five and a big smile.

My approach to Year 10 was vastly different. They were the 'top' class, so, in my eyes, required, and deserved, a more 'adult' approach. I would still be writing their starter on the board with my mug of coffee on my desk as they let themselves in, taking a seat wherever tickled their fancy that lesson. They would be loud and excitable, unpacking as they laughed and chatted with those around them. I'd be flouncing about from group to group, 'Come on Year 10; let's get started with what's up on the board.' I was more casual and conversational, walked quicker, talked louder, stood to the side and sipped my coffee, yelling out instructions over the noise. Then, when the bell rang for the end of the lesson, they would leave a trail of destruction in their wake. Chip packets, empty coke bottles, chairs untucked, crumbs on the floor and a defeated and flustered Miss English.

I simply had no idea where I was going right, and wrong.

Teaching had me bamboozled.

A bit of constructive feedback

Reflecting back on my approach to those two classes, the mistakes are plain as day. Although the Year 8 class was more 'challenging', I had crafted my non-verbal pedagogy and teaching presence in such a way that I was actively co-regulating with them every lesson, reinforcing the expectations, fostering an environment of calm and sending all of the right messages.

When I took a moment and a *breath* before the lesson had started, I was making sure I was *regulated* enough to do the work that needed to be done.

When I greeted them at the door and sent them in one by one, I was meeting them with my *stillness* and *calm*, shifting the energy from the playful playground to the more serious, productive and peaceful classroom environment.

I was watching my *pace*, moving slowly and stepping lightly, unintentionally modelling what I wanted from my classroom space, a space where my students and I felt safe and settled to learn.

I spoke softly and quietly, a gentle invitation for students to mirror that *volume and tone* right back to me.

I dropped my shoulders and stood up straight when I was addressing them, *holding myself* in a way that was credible, calm and controlled.

And I balanced this credible and composed persona with compassion and warmth, reinforcing that I was their teacher, I had boundaries, I had a job to do and so did they, but in a way that respected each child and sent messages that I cared deeply about them and their learning.

Contrastingly, I was sending the opposite messages in my Year 10 class. I was chatty, loud and conversational. I was more relaxed in my body, less postured, more casual, my pace was quick and frantic. I (wrongly) assumed that because they were the 'top' class, I wouldn't need to put the same work in as I did with my Year 8s.

These mistakes are some of the most common that I see with classroom management: non-verbal mixed messaging.

- I was pacing quickly about the room when I was trying to settle.
- I was passing things out when I wanted attention.
- I was talking loudly when I was expecting quiet.
- I was wanting calm but feeling and acting the opposite.
- I was wanting engagement but was teaching over the chatter.

Well, that was a lesson to learn.

All these non-verbal messages were the keys to the huge successes, and diabolical failures, I was having in my classroom that year. Although oblivious to it at the time, I was a living, breathing example of Michael Grinder's ENVoY (educational non-verbal yardsticks, 1995) concepts of the *approachable* and *credible* teaching strategies.

When we are *approachable*, our body language and movements are casual, loose, bubbly. We might be much more gestural with our hands, we will nod a lot more, we flip around the room being more engaging and expressive. We end our sentences with an upwards tone inviting comment and discussion, and our language may be less direct and more casual.

When we are using a more *credible* non-verbal approach, there is a focus on stillness, steadiness and slowness in our body language and movements. We are controlled and intentional, we breathe slow and deep, our hands are more still. Our tone is steady and our sentences end with a downwards inflection. Our language is direct and more formal.

Our ability to intentionally and strategically flip between these two 'modes' is crucial in crafting a teaching persona that non-verbally mitigates challenging behaviours. We may be more approachable during informal class discussions, small group instructions, one to ones with students, or outside a classroom. Whereas the credible would be more suited for whole-group instruction, transitions and more formal discussions.

By making some very small, yet very intentional changes in my non-verbal communication, I was able to turn things around with my Year 10 class immediately. I lined them up quietly, sent them in one by one, stood up the front quiet, composed and ready. One student yelled out, 'Miss English are you okay? What's wrong?' Another added, 'Yeah miss. You're acting weird' … before the entire class, without me saying a single word, quietly and calmly picked up a pen and started writing.

There is no magic wand for classroom management, but, if there was, these strategies would be the closest thing. The best thing about them? If you're ever in doubt, or in the midst of a lesson that feels completely out of control, just stop, take a deep breath and remind yourself of our next golden rule:

Be what you want to see.

Stop and ponder

Five questions to audit your non-verbal classroom communication:

1. When I am in a lesson, how do I feel? Am I calm and composed? Am I flustered and frantic? Am I breathing deep, or am I breathing shallow?
2. How am I inviting students into the room at the start of the lesson? *Is what I am saying and how I am saying it credible or approachable?*
3. Where do I stand when I am addressing the class? Is it the same each time? Is it front and centre or off to the side?
4. When I am giving teacher-led instruction, how am I 'holding myself'? Am I standing up straight or am I slouching? Am I still, or am I moving around and shifting my weight?
5. If I am expecting students to be quietly working, how am I moving around the room? Am I pacing quickly or moving slowly? Having loud conversations or keeping things at a whisper?

Part 2: Calmly *addressing* challenging behaviour

Your use of all the self-regulation and non-verbal strategies from Part 1 will undoubtedly lead to a reduction in dysregulated behaviours.

However, no matter how calm we are or how on-point our teaching presence is, whether we do absolutely everything right or not, we can never eliminate challenging behaviour. After all, let's not forget what business we are in: working with perfectly imperfect humans.

When challenging behaviour *does* surface in front of a class of onlookers, the heat of the moment can feel like a minefield to navigate. You can't let that student speak to you like that in front of the rest of the class? You surely must set an example? What message would that send to the others? That is a lot of pressure when we are one on 30, so a battle of egos ensues. A battle that cannot be won.

So, you need an approach that calmly and effectively addresses the behaviour, while sending messages to the class that you will be consistent in your expectations. An approach that avoids the battle and allows you to quickly get back to the job that you have at hand – teaching the class.

The goal

If we take a student who is already in a dysregulated state and we publicly threaten them or yell at them, we move ourselves further away from our number one goal: de-escalation!

What we don't need to do in the middle of a lesson is 'teach that student a lesson'. We don't need to resolve things right then and there, we don't need to change their behaviour in the long run and we don't need to dish out consequences.

Yes, I can hear a collective sigh of relief. Behaviour is immensely complex; we are simply not able to deal with everything then and there in the moment. Consider this your permission slip to address what is happening in that room in the best way you can, so you can crack on with the teaching and learning.

If we don't need to resolve behaviour in the moment, then what *should* we be doing?

Part 2 of this Pillar will give you a step-by-step of what to do about behaviour in the midst of the storm. All these decisions we make (and there are hundreds, if not thousands, of micro-decisions we make a day) can either escalate or de-escalate.

No matter what is happening, no matter how disrespectful or disruptive the behaviour is, our ultimate goal in the heat of the moment *must be* to quickly and calmly de-escalate. Another reminder of how crucial our own regulation is before stepping into that room.

Stop and ponder

Imagine for a moment that you notice that a student is off-task, using their phone, disrupting others, getting restless, whatever the challenging behaviour might be. You march towards them, stand over them, bark orders at them publicly.

(Continued)

What might the impact be?
Will they respect you?
Listen to you?
Are you doing what you are asking them to do?

Certainly not. Hello escalation! Hello fight or flight! Hello lose–lose! Not only will it escalate the behaviour in the moment, but also in the lessons to follow. Goodbye even more teaching time!

So, what do we do instead?

Follow the *six Ps of calm classroom management*. This response allows us to work *with* the student and behaviour more fluidly, not *against* it … just as you can't stop a torrent of water coming downstream, but you can redirect it gently, slowly, little by little.

Your six Ps of calm classroom management

The six Ps are a powerful set of pedagogical strategies that allow teachers to de-escalate behaviour and reinforce expectations in a way that is non-confrontational. Once you have the six Ps hardwired into your everyday pedagogy and presence, this will be your golden ticket to fostering a calm classroom environment and paving the way for authentic buy-in and change.

Although they are a toolbox of strategies you can draw from individually when needed, when used together they become a powerful roadmap to effectively address some of the most common and frustrating classroom management challenges we face.

Six stops to addressing and resolving challenging classroom behaviour

Stop #1: Pause

A strategically placed pause effectively models attention and silence, and can be very effective when:

- done mid-sentence; just a little short and sharp jolt when you're trying to stop that chatter from erupting;
- when you're trying to get the whole class back on track.

Image 2.4   Our calm classroom management toolbox

The success of this strategy hinges on your ability to be patient, calm and composed. It is easy to lose confidence and cut the pause short, but teaching over the chatter will only exacerbate low-level behaviours. Instead, continue to model the expectation of silence and refrain from the old classic, 'It's not my time you're wasting'. Your class may initially take a bit of time to get used to responding to this non-verbal, but don't lose faith. Use this consistently and your students will start reading this cue like a book.

What it looks like: Being in 'credible' mode. Take a breath, stand straight front and centre, and be still.

Stop #2: Pace

When pausing doesn't put out the spot-fire, it's time to approach the behaviour head on.

Be warned, as easily as this step can extinguish the fire, it can also dump fuel over it.

If you're storming up to a student, you might find yourself on the receiving end of a fight, flight or freeze response. This is why, just like all the strategies in this road-map, approaching your students requires you to be regulated and calm. If you yourself are escalated from the behaviour in your classroom, you're much less likely to be strategic, calm and composed when approaching the very student who is pressing those buttons.

This isn't just relevant for when you're in the middle of whole-class instruction either; it can be used for group work when students are a bit off-task and has come in handy in almost every single assembly I have supervised.

What it looks like: Simply moving from where you are to where the student is who needs to be addressed, calmly, slowly and credibly.

Stop #3: Position

Remember, our goal is de-escalation so we can get back to teaching the lesson. As such, when addressing our students, we need to consciously position ourselves in a way that is non-confrontational.

What it looks like: When you're addressing student behaviour, instead of standing up and looking down, or being directly in front of a student demanding eye contact (all confrontational positions), crouch down next to them. This position is non-confrontational and places you in the perfect position for the next step of the roadmap.

We can also use our position strategically when we are walking around support-ing during individual or group tasks, or supervising assemblies and examinations. Just through our presence near a student, we can gently redirect and get them back on track.

Stop #4: Privacy

How we address our students can be the difference between an agreeable nod and a big 'f you'.

Behaviour is deeply personal, and addressing it publicly can cause deep shame and embarrassment. When we call out students in front of their peers, we are poten-tially triggering an unwinnable war of words; a battle that both the teacher and the student will continue to escalate in order to save face and regain some semblance of control. Avoid this at all costs by keeping any discussion on behaviour as private as the space will allow.

What it looks like: Using our position to be next to a student, touch base and quietly give them very clear, concise and calm instructions.

When we speak to them in a quiet, private voice, we are not only avoiding the battle, but our calm response is helping us to actively co-regulate with them. This can immediately disarm students and stop those behaviours in their tracks.

Stop #5: Plan

Despite our best efforts, it is inevitable that students will sometimes still flat out refuse to follow our instructions. Instead of getting into a verbal back and forth in front of the class, provide explicit instructions for students about their behaviour and then move away.

When we do this, we are removing that instant authoritative action while still setting limits and reinforcing boundaries. It is a win–win; the rest of the class see you addressing it, so you don't lose face, and you won't spend the next ten minutes fighting that student to do what you're asking. They know what that logical consequence will be, you've explained it calmly and you feel empowered because you know there is a plan to follow it up.

What it looks like: Provide a 'plan' in a private and calm voice:

- reinforce what you expect of them and what two options they have;
- tell them what the follow-up will be and then move away again slowly to let them make their choice;
- follow up on anything at a more appropriate time.

Stop #6: Pursue

There are going to be students who don't follow the plan. They will continue to display challenging or disruptive behaviour.

When this happens, don't fret, there is a next step. In the following pillar I will be giving you the tools you need to authentically resolve the behaviours that require a bit more follow-up.

The six Ps in action

The nuances when it comes to classroom behaviour are endless. That is why the six Ps are designed to be highly adaptable to a wide range of challenges in the classroom (and beyond). The following scenarios contextualise these strategies and support you to build your confidence in choosing the right approach to what is playing out in front of you.

For the purposes of running through the whole roadmap, I have written these scenarios as if there is resistance at every step. In reality, a lot of behaviours will be nipped in the bud before escalating the response right up to the final P.

Scenario 1: A whole-school assembly

You are supervising students during a whole-school assembly. As a teacher begins presenting different awards and calling out names, one of your students starts saying inappropriate things audibly for those around them. Others begin laughing, shifting about, getting unsettled and ready to join in on the fun. You know that if you don't address this, it is going to cause quite the stir.

Pause: You move yourself towards where the students are and pause for a moment, using your gaze and credible body language to try to non-verbally put out the spot-fire.

Pace: The student calling things out sees you and says, 'What miss?' confrontationally, as the students around whip their heads your way. You take a breath and slowly and calmly move towards him.

Position: You position yourself slightly next to/behind the student and kneel down, a position that is non-confrontational. You keep your eyes to the front, modelling the expectation of watching the assembly.

Privacy: You make sure you keep your voice very low, almost at a whisper to not draw more attention. You remind the student of the expectations of being in an assembly.

'I am just going to remind you that when we are in an assembly, we aren't the ones that are talking.'
If they start to settle: non-verbal recognition such as a thumbs up.
If they don't: move onto a plan.

Plan: The student scoffs, so you provide them with a plan and options (shown below), stand up slowly, walk to the side of the row but maintain proximity so they know you are monitoring to see what option they will choose.

'You have two options, sit quietly, and watch the rest of the assembly, or if you think that might be a challenge, you can come and sit next to me up the back here and we can discuss more after. I will be just over there keeping an eye out to see what you choose to do.'

As this scenario is in the middle of an assembly, the goal would be to de-escalate the situation while keeping instructions and conversations to an absolute minimum to not cause a scene. Due to this, the example doesn't allow for any back and forth, but provides very concise and explicit instructions, and a very clear plan if the student continues to refuse. It is very important to deliver that message in a way that is non-confrontational, so eyes to the front, voice credible, calm and just delivering the facts.

Scenario 2: Phone use

You are giving the whole class instructions at the start of the lesson and there is one student sitting at the back who is on their phone. You catch their eye and motion for them to put it away. They look at you, shake their head, look back down at their phone and keep doing what they were doing.

Pause: You pause for just a moment to see if they will make a different decision. You keep silent, body still. They don't put it away, so you move to the next step.

Pace: Very slowly you make your way over to where the student is. You keep yourself controlled and calm to not inflame the situation.

Position: You position yourself next to the student and kneel down.

Privacy: You make sure you keep your voice very low, almost at a whisper, to ensure you aren't triggering that fight or flight response. This will give you the maximum amount of buy-in with the student.

'Are you okay? I can see you are distracted at the moment. You know we don't use our phones in class time. What do you think I am going to ask you to do?'
If they put it away: *'Thank you, that was a good choice.'*
If they don't: move onto plan.

Plan: You make a plan with the student (shown below) so you are able to address the behaviour, while still giving yourself an 'out'. Then, you walk away and allow that student to make their own choice without having a reason to lock horns with you.
'You know that if we can't use our phones responsibly that we need to hand them in in the morning. This is your choice, but I am going to walk away now because I need to go and teach the rest of this lesson. I will be keeping an eye to see if you are able to pop that away for me in the next 30 seconds and get back on track, okay?'

Scenario 3: Work refusal

A student in your class rarely does any work and is incredibly challenging to motivate. This lesson is important as the rest of the learning for the week hinges upon it, but they are sitting there with their head on their desk yet again. **Pause** is not relevant, so ...

(Continued)

Pace: You approach the student slowly and calmly.

Position: You kneel beside them. They don't engage with you and keep their head down.

Privacy: You first connect with the student and see if they are okay. They nod and you get curious about why they aren't completing any of the work.

'Are you okay? I can see you are having a bit of trouble getting started on the work. Is there anything that I should know? Is there something with the work that I can help with?'

Plan: The student stated that everything was fine, that they just didn't want to do the work because it was stressing them out. You plan for them to get three of the questions done in the time they have left and that you would have a talk with them after about how much work they are missing out on.

'I am glad that everything is okay, but I am worried that the work is stressing you out. What I think a good plan would be, now that time is running out, is just to get these last three questions done because they are the most important ones. I will keep an eye out to see how you get on with that, but I think it would be a good idea for us to catch up about this after either way to see what we can do to make this less stressful for you.'

There are many reasons why students will refuse to complete their work, and very rarely is it just 'laziness'. Sometimes students will mask their confusion or lack of confidence to complete the work by saying it is boring or that they don't feel like doing it. Other students may struggle to begin the work because they are dysregulated and are not able to access their 'thinking brain' for learning.

Even if it is that student being a little 'lazy', there's always a reason for that too. Think back to the last time you felt like you just couldn't bring yourself to tackle work. Was it because you were lazy or incompetent, or was it because you felt overwhelmed, swamped, or exhausted? Whatever the reason is for work refusal, it is important to approach it with curiosity and compassion. This ultimately gives you the best chance possible of resolving things effectively.

Scenario 4: Inappropriate comments

You are in the middle of a lesson and students are working in groups on an activity. As you walk around the room, you overhear one group off-task. One of the boys makes a comment to the rest of the group 'I would just tell my girlfriend to get in the kitchen and make me a sandwich,' as the others burst into laughter. You skip the **pause** because when something inappropriate has been said, it always needs to be verbally addressed. This is not the time to put out the spot-fire and move on! You make your way over to the group.

Position: You kneel next to the student who made the comment.

Privacy: You make sure to keep your voice low so only him and the group that were involved in the discussion can hear. You name the language for what it is, sexist and misogynistic, and express that it is harmful. Remain calm and be sure to label the language rather than the student. The focus in these circumstances should always be on education.

'Do you know that what you just said was a very sexist thing to say and is very harmful? Do you know what sexism is? Can you explain that to me?'

Plan: The student says they know what sexism is; however, when they try to explain it, it is clear they don't understand. You then plan with the student to discuss it further after the lesson. You want to make sure that student knows why it was a harmful thing to say, and by addressing it seriously you are communicating that to the rest of the class too.

'Peter, it sounds like you really didn't know why it was a harmful thing to say; you aren't in trouble, I just really would like for you to stay back after the lesson because it is really important that we have a bit more of a chat about this.'

When students say things that are harmful and discriminatory, it is crucial that we address this seriously. Every single student deserves to feel safe in our classrooms. It can be a very difficult thing to navigate, but by naming the behaviour immediately, and focusing on education rather than shame, we can meaningfully address this, get buy-in from the student and proactively minimise these comments in future.

Pillar 2 at a glance

- **The most crucial classroom management resource at our disposal is us.** We are the conductor of the energy in our classrooms. Our ability to remain calm and regulated is our golden ticket to mitigating challenging classroom behaviour (particularly low-level behaviour). Pausing, taking a breath and getting curious are three actionable steps in supporting us to regulate in stressful classroom circumstances.

(Continued)

- **Be what you want to see**. We are constantly sending non-verbal messages to our students; very often these messages conflict with what we are requiring and expecting from our students. Follow the golden rule: 'be what you want to see', and focus on modelling the calm that you want from your students in return.
- **A strong teaching presence can be strategically crafted through non-verbal communication.** When we focus on our pace, how we hold ourselves and the volume and tone of what we are saying, we can significantly reduce and de-escalate challenging behaviours in our classroom.
- **De-escalation needs to be our number one goal when addressing classroom behaviours**. We do this through calmly using the six Ps of calm classroom management: pause, pace, position, privacy, plan and pursue. These six Ps are non-confrontational and allow us to get back to the teaching as quickly as possible.

Digging deeper

Listen in:

Hear me talk through the how-to of addressing inappropriate connects on Episode 27 of The Unteachables Podcast: *Addressing Misogyny (and Other Damaging Comments) in the Classroom: Your Step-by-Step Guide.*

Add to your bookshelf:

Choice Theory: A New Psychology of Personal Freedom, William Glasser (New York: Harper Collins, 1998).
ENVoY: Your Personal Guide to Classroom Management, Michael Grinder (Battle Ground, WA: Michael Grinder & Associates, 1995).

PILLAR 3
Be Compassionate

For teachers to move away from harmful exclusionary practices, they need more than just a strong 'why' and compassion for their students; they need tangible, actionable and compassionate pedagogy.

Groundhog day

I used to say, as do many others, 'I want to be the teacher that I needed when I was at school.' It is admirable, it is a strong 'why' and it is all well and good until we get into the profession and the behaviours hit us like a tonne of bricks.

I quickly became frustrated and jaded by the sheer multitude and severity of class-room behaviours, my 'why' dwindling with each torturously slow minute ... 75 to go. 40 to go. 39 to go. The relief of surviving another lesson was palpable.

Then the students would leave as they came, with a trail of destruction in their wake. It was a battlefield of upturned chairs on a garbage-strewn carpet, unidentifi-able crumbs firmly compacted into the ground, topped by hundreds of teeny pieces of untouched classwork. As I went about the business of the clean-up, moving between the rows of tables, pouring drops of water as I went in a poor attempt to rub off the oodles of doodles, the last thing I was thinking was 'Oh, these poor vulnerable students'.

I had firmly lost my way. Despite a solid foundation of good intentions and chal-lenging school experiences of my own, I found myself resenting many of my students. One most of all.

James was the ringleader of the chaos that ensued in room 25. His 'I don't give a crap I'll do what I want' attitude was infectious, boosting the confidence of the class to follow suit. His reintegration after spending a significant amount of time at a pupil referral unit for violent and antisocial behaviours injected a new level of disruption in an already unmanageable space. I braced myself for impact every lesson, crossing my fingers in the hopes he wouldn't show up. But, of course, he did. He never took a day off.

'I need to teach him a lesson,' I thought. After all, this boy was naughty, disre-spectful and nasty. He didn't care about his peers, his learning, his future and he was actively stealing the opportunity to learn from the other students.

So, I gave him the consequences I thought he deserved, the consequences that I felt might finally snap him out of it. They say the only certainties in life are death and taxes. Well, at this time in my career there was a third certainty: each day that I taught James, come recess or lunch he'd be back in my room staring at the wall. Then, like Groundhog Day, he would return the next lesson more disruptive, more dysregulated and more unteachable than ever before.

On the cycle would go.

One day we had a whole staff meeting about James, his behaviours and what we could do as a staff team to support him (and us). I was all pumped up and ready to advocate for his exclusion, whether it be temporary or permanent. I needed a break, before I broke. But in this meeting things shifted. We learnt that his life had been punctuated by a series of events that had left him broken, discarded, lost and alone. We learnt that he was very recently back in the care of his parents after four disjointed years in foster care. We heard of police and child services involvement from birth due to severe neglect.

The veil was lifted, a stark reminder of the third golden rule:

Happy students are rarely disengaged and destructive students.

No wonder James responded to me in the way he did. If the people who were supposed to unconditionally love and protect him were a source of deep pain, then why would he have any reason to trust me?

Especially considering I hadn't given him a reason to trust me.

In fact, it was the very opposite.

He didn't stand a chance walking through my classroom door.

They don't stand a chance, and neither do we

When I say that James didn't stand a chance walking into room 25, it wasn't because of his behaviours, nor was it his lack of engagement. It was because of how deeply ingrained my beliefs, assumptions and biases about him were.

I told myself so many things. He is rude. He is disruptive. He is disrespectful. He doesn't care about his learning. He is lazy. He is going to derail the lesson. He is going to get himself sent out of the room; in fact, 'I bet he won't last ten minutes.'

All these things shaped the way that I approached James. I braced myself, expecting it, believing he was choosing this. Believing that if he just felt the consequences of his actions, if I took away enough of the remaining joy he had in his school day, he would magically decide to behave better. All of which, of course, was happening on an unconscious level. I was desperately falling back on my 'inherited' classroom management strategies. Strategies that, although punitive, I felt were my best chance of getting back in the driver's seat, with two hands on the steering wheel.

What was actually happening was the polar opposite. At the very core of our behaviour management system is the idea that punishments will deter future mis-behaviour; however, studies show that 'rather than reducing the likelihood of disruption, school suspension in general appears to predict higher future rates of misbehaviour and suspension among those students who are suspended' (APA, 2008, p. 854). Ironically, the students who these consequences are designed for, students like James, are the ones who are the least likely to respond to them.

Worse than these strategies simply not working ...

When we monitor and address behaviour publicly: we potentially increase the stress response for every single student in our classroom, simultaneously increasing fight, flight, or freeze behaviours. We might be getting compliance, but that compliance is out of the fear of being publicly named and shamed. The students who struggle the most are at an instant disadvantage as it's often from a lack of skill, not will, that they are not able to comply. It's also not good news for learning, either. Remember that if the brain's on high alert, the 'feeling' brain is in charge, making it harder for all of those 'thinking' brain functions to be accessed.

When we take away their break times: it is not teaching them the skills they need to change the behaviours that got them there in the first place, unless, of course, you are using this time for restorative work.

The students who get detentions are constantly getting detentions. They become numb to it, they don't care about it and, eventually, they say (with their words, or actions), 'Nope, not happening', further disengaging and disconnecting from us and their education.

When we send them out of the room: exclusion is the opposite of what students who exhibit the most challenging behaviours need to progress – connection. It per-petuates all the negative beliefs a student holds about themselves: 'I am unworthy, I am unlovable, I am undeserving' and reinforces that school is not a place of safety, care and concern. Of course, there are times where work outside the classroom space is appropriate and needs to be done; however, the way we approach and organise this matters.

When we yell and threaten: confrontation immediately escalates the nervous sys-tem and pumps out the adrenaline students need to either fight you, or flee from you. It has the potential to create a disastrous lose–lose scenario, with students feeling the need to save face in front of their peers – leaving us locking horns and escalat-ing things beyond the point of no return.

Stop and ponder

Use the following six questions to openly and honestly reflect on a recent classroom management challenge. This is a judgement-free zone! It's an opportunity to get curious about the conscious and unconscious decisions that you make, and how this might be shaping the culture of your classroom.

1. What was the behaviour? How did you respond in the moment?
2. Did the way you approached the behaviour support regulation and connection, or further dysregulation and disconnection?
3. Did you see a de-escalation or an escalation of the challenging behaviour in the moment? Why do you think this was?
4. What messages do you think your response to this behaviour sent to that student?
5. If you were to put your 'behaviour detective' hat on now and get a bit curious, what questions might you ask yourself and what insights might you gain?
6. What kind of classroom culture did this response contribute to creating? Did it foster an environment of felt safety, care and concern? Or the opposite?

Do the crime, do the time!

Putting all of the above very plainly, making school more miserable for students *can* never, and *will* never, create positive change.

The behaviour cycle simply continues; detention after detention, suspension after suspension, eventually ending in expulsion from mainstream education: a cycle that perpetuates the school to prison pipeline, a phenomenon which describes the way in which punitive school behaviour systems contribute to an increase in a young person's likelihood for future criminality and susceptibility to exploitation.

It's easy to understand why; instead of providing students opportunities for connection and learning, students who are caught in the pipeline are increasingly disconnected and isolated. This leads to what the IPPR report *Making the Difference* describes as a cycle of 'social immobility', leading to poor outcomes that 'stretch across a range of social dimensions including: health, qualifications, employment, and criminality' (Gill, 2017, p. 21). In fact, the Commission on Young Lives report revealed that 63 per cent of prisoners had been temporarily excluded and 42 per cent had been permanently excluded while at school (Commission on Young Lives, 2022).

The following image is adapted from a powerful campaign organised by South London school students called 'Education Not Exclusion'. In 2018 on GCSE results day, they took to the underground replacing tube maps with 'School to Prison Line' stickers, raising awareness around the impact of school exclusions.

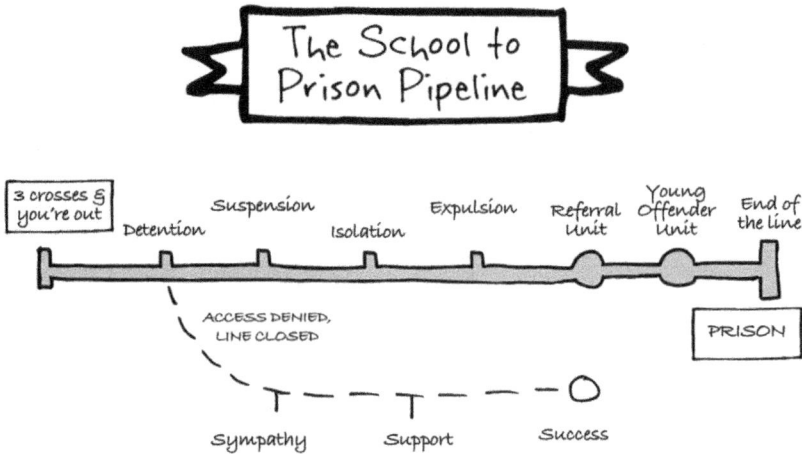

Image 3.1   The school to prison pipeline

Punitive behaviour management approaches in schools are not just failing students, but also are perpetuating systemic racism and marginalising societies most vulnerable. Certain demographics of students are disproportionately affected by the system. The IPPR report reveals that there are several risk factors, or 'vulnerabilities', that increase the likelihood of children being excluded, including 'living in poverty, experiencing abuse and neglect at home, having a learning difficulty, having low attainment in school, and suffering from a mental health condition' (Gill, 2017, p. 16). As well as this, in pupil referral units in England, 'boys of black Caribbean heritage … are significantly overrepresented' (Perera, 2020, p. 6), putting them on a one-way trip down the pipeline. This can be explained by a number of factors such as institutional racism, low expectations of black students, a lack of effective staff training and diversity and race issues in staffing and beyond (Demie, 2019).

As students become increasingly isolated from their education, they become far more vulnerable to exploitation. The report *Counting Lives: Responding to Children who are Criminally Exploited* (Turner et al., 2019) explores the disturbing prevalence of criminal gangs targeting, grooming and exploiting vulnerable youth who are in desperate need of love and belonging, as young as seven or eight years old – many of whom are coerced into a life of crime after being excluded from mainstream education.

There is a lot that needs to be done systematically to break this cycle – a cycle deeply embedded into the bones of our school discipline systems; a cycle that, let's be honest, isn't only making things worse for our students, but also making things far harder for us as teachers. This book, however, isn't about taking on the mammoth task of addressing and resolving the deep and systemic issues present; it is about what we can immediately control when we walk through those school gates. How, through a deeper awareness of the inequalities that exist, a genuine reflection on our own biases and assumptions, and an authentic and compassionate approach to discipline, we can turn our classrooms into islands of safety and inclusion for every single student.

Our students need to be disciplined

James needed discipline. However, there had already been detentions, time spent at a pupil referral unit, police involvement for assaults and thefts. What more could I dish out that hadn't already been experienced in vain?

The discipline he needed, the true discipline, was not what I understood it to be. Lorraine Fox sums up the misconception that:

> the terms discipline, punishment, and consequences are often used in discussion, and consequently in practice, as if they were the same things. They are not. … The literal meaning of the term 'to discipline' is to teach … If we intervene with behaviour with any intent other than to teach, we are not administering true discipline.

(Fox, 2005)

Yet if you said that to me at the time, my response would have been, 'Well, what about the students who want to learn, students who deserve a classroom free from this nonsense?'. I wouldn't have blamed me, nor do I blame teachers who feel this way. The teacher guilt attached to watching the room descend into chaos while the compliant students sit there wide-eyed, waiting for you to impart your knowledge, is all too real. Removing disruptive students from the classroom feels like a logical response from teachers who want to be able to get back to what they got into the profession to do, teach. However, the data has shown that this has an opposite effect on a classroom climate, and that 'schools with higher rates of school suspension and expulsion appear to have less satisfactory ratings of school climate … and spend a disproportionate amount of time on disciplinary matters' (APA, 2008, p. 854).

So, what can frustrated, disillusioned, overworked, under resourced and burnt-out educators who are plagued with a torrent of challenging classroom behaviours actually *do*?

What is true discipline?

There came a time in my early career where I felt I had nailed the classroom management game. Most of my students knew what to expect; anybody who spoke out of turn would add a minute on the board for the whole class to make up at lunch. I often had my class doing the dirty work for me, shushing their peers in frustration. Nobody wanted to lose their lunch, so I inadvertently created an army of 'compliance keepers'.

Instead of inspiring quality learning, camouflaged by compliance was shame, disconnection, fear and disengagement. I had classes full of compliant students, but not necessarily students who were happy, engaged, inspired or psychologically safe. The students who didn't have the skills to comply often voted with their feet and simply left, putting me yet another three steps back with their behaviour and rapport.

Rather than an extrinsic classroom management approach that aims to control behaviour through force, fear and coercion, true discipline demands that we gain buy-in. We reinforce expectations and boundaries with compassion. We teach them to know better, and do better, through respectful and strategic dialogue. We provide them with consequences, but ones that are fair, equitable and make sense to the student and the behaviour. It is through true discipline that we can work *with* our students, rather than *against* them.

Real discipline in action

Although a more restorative approach does not ignore the need for consequences, it differs from a traditional approach in that they have a focus on accountability, reflection, restoration, learning and, ultimately, authentically addressing the underlying causes of behaviour – in essence, using the challenge as an opportunity to teach the student, therefore reducing the reason for that consequence over time.

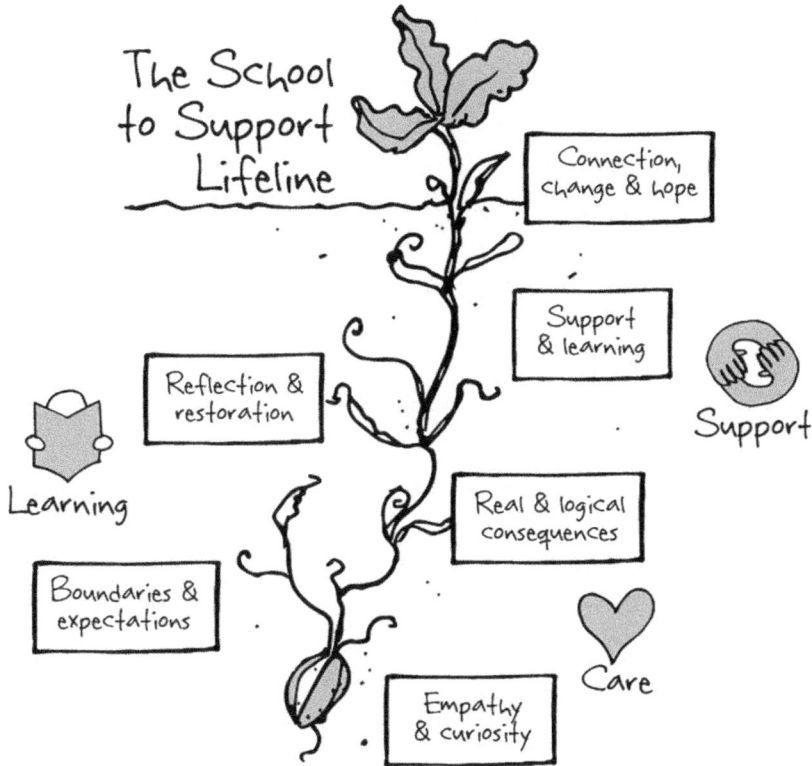

Image 3.2   The school to support lifeline

With this approach to resolving challenges, behaviour is managed through respect, support, collaboration and discussion. It supports our young people to learn, to make different choices, to engage in consequences that make sense to them, that they can buy into.

Jane Nelson's three Rs of logical consequences provides an easy framework for what constitutes a suitable consequence. You can ask yourself:

- is the consequence *related* to the behaviour?
- is the consequence *respectful*?
- is the consequence *reasonable*?

Nelson expresses that if any of these three Rs are missing, it cannot be classified as a logical consequence. The following are five foundational consequences I use as a basis in my classroom practice. Rather than a punitive 'one size fits all', they are focused on authentically righting the wrong, and encouraging accountability through support and collaboration. Unlike punitive punishments, they mitigate future challenges as they gain maximum buy-in with students.

- You break something, you help fix it.
- You mess it up, you clean it.
- You have an argument or a fight, you engage in a conflict resolution.
- You had a challenging lesson, you discuss why and make a plan for next time.
- You act in a way that is harmful, you take responsibility and make it right.

So, logical consequences for students can be as simple as making attempts to fix what has been damaged. Whether it's helping screw a table back together, talking through a conflict, reflecting on the harm that was done, or teaching them to make a different choice, these consequences are working on an intrinsic level to create change.

However, these consequences do not work in isolation. After all, getting a student to clean up a mess is not going to stop another mess from happening. Resolving behavioural challenges is a lot more than the consequence itself; the true magic of discipline lies in the pedagogy surrounding it. If we just slap on a consequence, we can't expect to have understanding, growth, reflection and real accountability. If we want these things (spoiler alert, we do), we must understand that the pedagogical journey to the consequence matters far more than the consequence itself.

Once you have calmly mitigated and de-escalated behaviours, you now need to seize the opportunity and follow up. Yes, I said opportunity! Challenging behaviours open up a doorway to supporting our students to develop a plethora of social and emotional skills, to know better and do better, and to even strengthen that all-important rapport. This is where Stop 3 on our journey to calmly mitigating and addressing challenging behaviour comes in, the *transformative talks*.

Transformative talks

There are a lot of misconceptions about an approach that is restorative rather than punitive. There is a belief that students 'get away with their behaviour' or that it is a 'soft approach'. It is the opposite. It requires a greater deal of accountability and reflection.

We aren't excusing or ignoring behaviour. And, when approached correctly, teachers are ultimately more empowered, more skilled and more effective in working with all of their students (not just the more challenging ones).

Transformative talks are the bread and butter of this approach.

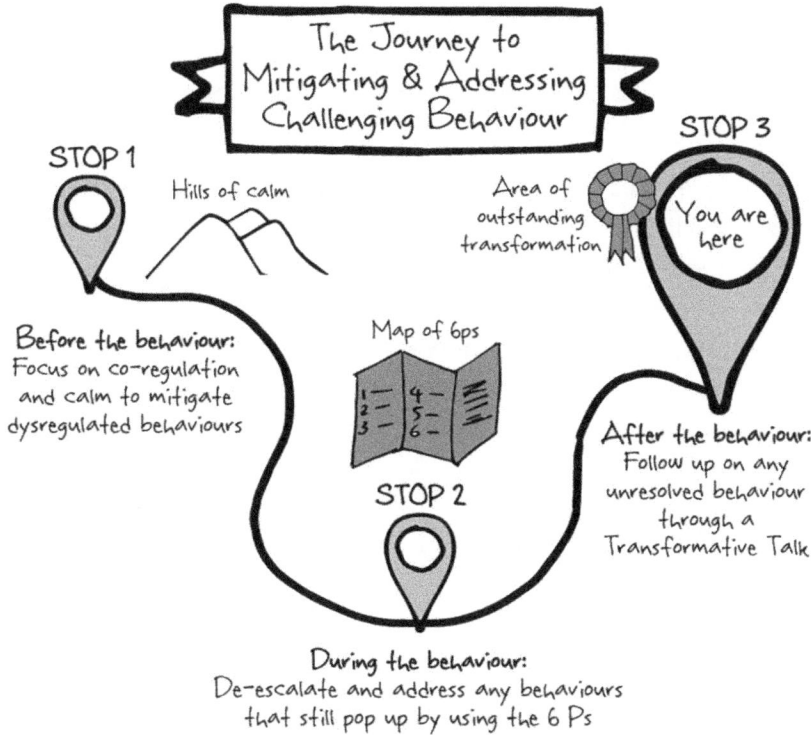

The Journey to Mitigating & Addressing Challenging Behaviour

STOP 1

Hills of calm

STOP 3

Area of outstanding transformation

You are here

Before the behaviour:
Focus on co-regulation and calm to mitigate dysregulated behaviours

Map of 6ps

1 —   4 —
2 —   5 —
3 —   6 —

After the behaviour:
Follow up on any unresolved behaviour through a Transformative Talk

STOP 2

During the behaviour:
De-escalate and address any behaviours that still pop up by using the 6 Ps

Image 3.3   The journey to mitigating and addressing challenging behaviour

What are they?

Achieving behaviour change hinges on our ability to strategically engage students in dialogue where we discuss concerns, resolve challenges and restore relationships. These discussions are simply opportunities to teach, support, connect and plan.

Transformative talks come in all shapes and sizes; they can be simple, casual, quick and to the point, or can require more in-depth planning and a substantial amount of time. This depends on the unique circumstances and context of the behaviour itself.

Not too dissimilar to restorative justice conversations, I have adapted transformative talks specifically for busy teachers in the context of resolving classroom challenges. They provide a level of flexibility which enables teachers to conduct these discussions in relation to a wide range of issues, meaningfully resolving challenging behaviours of all kinds.

Engaging in transformative talk

When we are engaging in a transformative talk, the goals are to:

- connect, listen and invest in the relationship (more on investments later);
- reflect on the event/behaviour, unpack the harm caused and support students to take accountability;
- reinforce your expectations and boundaries;
- dig into the *why* behind the behaviour;
- decide on an appropriate consequence with the student;
- meaningfully resolve things for a fresh start.

When to use them

Resolve: any time you believe that a student's behaviour in class was not resolved to your satisfaction in the moment, or if it was successfully de-escalated but you think it requires further addressing.

Reinforce: when you want to emphasise expectations or boundaries for ongoing behavioural concerns.

Respond: when a student is struggling with regulation/work/engagement and you want to explore this and support them to make some progress.

How to use them

The following structure of the discussion works for transformative talks in all situations, whether you have a quick, to the point, informal chat with a student, or if there is a more lengthy and serious discussion that is required.

You also don't need to strictly stick to this structure. As you build your confidence and hardwire those skills, you will be able to approach this in a more fluid and natural way. This structure simply provides you with an understanding around how to get to the heart of the behaviour, raise responsibility and accountability with students, and ensure you are finishing the conversation with a proactive plan forward and a meaningful consequence.

Image 3.4 Transformative talks at a glance

Step 1: Tell our stories, getting curious and checking in

Always start by connecting and coming from a place of care and concern. Approaching students from a place of understanding and compassion always ensures you get the most buy-in. Without the buy-in, you're not going to get the level of vulnerability and reflection needed to create real change.

You might start with these types of things.

- Come have a quick chat. Is everything okay?
- Today was a bit of a tough one? Is there anything I need to be aware of?
- That was a very difficult lesson/situation; can you explain what was going on for you?
- What were you thinking and feeling at the time?
- Can you tell me what happened in your own words?

- What was the trigger/catalyst/cause?
- What happened after that?
- Can I explain what I saw at the time? (If necessary to get back on track.)

Step 2: Explore and acknowledge the harm

Once you are confident that you have got to the heart of what occurred and the potential reasons behind it, it is time to unpack the challenge itself and the harm that was caused (whether it is harm to self or others). You cannot move on from this part unless the student has taken accountability for the harm that has been caused. If there is hesitancy and you're not getting to where you need to be, it can be useful to put a pause on the conversation and revisit this again once the dust has settled.

You could do this through guiding the conversation in the following ways.

- Do you understand why the things you said are serious and not okay? Can you explain that to me in your own words?
- Who do you think these comments and behaviours hurt and how? Who do you think might have been hurt by them when you said them? How might you make that right?
- What was the impact on me/the class/your own learning?
- Was what happened helpful or unhelpful? To whom?
- Was this benefitting your learning? Why? Why not?
- Did that make whatever was going on for you better or worse?
- How do you think they might be feeling right now?

Step 3: Plan for restoration and change

The goal for this step is to teach students the skills they need to make change, whether that be a different choice, a regulation strategy, or education around something that they have done or said. It is also the time where you deliver the consequence (when necessary or appropriate). However, if we simply dictate this to them, we are missing the opportunity to collaborate and decide on the best way to move forward.

It is important to note that you won't see anything prompting an apology from a student. This is because unless the apology is genuine it does not support the individual that was harmed and is often an easy out for students who have done the harming.

Without the work around the apology, authentic development and restoration doesn't occur.

- What might we do next time this happens?
- Can we think of some strategies for when you are feeling like this?
- What do you think is needed to make things right? May I offer suggestions also? Have a look at this list here.
- What do you think about what they have just said?
- Is there anything you think they need to hear to be able to move forward?
- What do you think you might need to do differently next time?
- Even if you didn't mean it, another person's feelings were hurt. When you are hurt, what do you need?

A little tip: I keep a visual copy of my foundational consequences handy to use during these chats as a resource called 'Ideas for making things right'. This helps to prompt students to choose a consequence that is the most logical for themselves. When they can decide on the best way to restore the harm done, it is far more meaningful than it being dictated to them.

Pursue: Revisiting our challenging behaviour scenarios

Take the following as a general example of the language we might use with our students to resolve the challenges that pop up, rather than an exact 'to do'. Your relationship with the student, the context of the behaviour, the student's history, the student's needs and every other unique factor will determine the response that you take.

As long as you tick off the goals of the discussion and there is genuine reflection and learning, your transformative talk has hit the mark.

Scenario 1: Assembly

You were supervising a whole-school assembly when a student called out inappropriate things. You followed the six Ps, but, despite giving them a plan to sit quietly and watch the rest of the assembly, they continued escalating with loud and rude comments.

(Continued)

You get them to sit at the back with you for the remainder of the assembly and once it is over you follow the plan you made and have a transformative talk about their behaviour.

Step 1: Tell our stories, getting curious and checking in.

- That assembly was a very difficult one; why do you think I needed you to come and sit back here with me?
- Yes, exactly, thank you for acknowledging that.

Step 2: Explore and acknowledge the harm.

- When you were yelling those things out, what do you think the impact might have been?
- Can you explain to me why this was not a helpful/kind thing to be doing?
- Who else might that have been impacting?

Step 3: Plan for restoration and change.

- Can you think of why it was hard for you to settle in this assembly?
- Next time we have an assembly, what can you do differently?
- That's a great plan, well done. In the next assembly, you will come and sit with me. That way, you can let me know if you are feeling restless and I will be able to help you either have a time out, or manage a little better.

Scenario 2: Phone out

You were giving the whole class instructions and a student was on their phone. After giving them a plan to put it away, they refused and spent the rest of the lesson using it.

Step 1: Tell our stories, getting curious and checking in.

- Is there anything I need to know? Can you explain what was going on for you during the lesson that made you want to be on your phone?

Step 2: Explore and acknowledge the harm.

- Do you know why I asked you to put your phone away and why I can't have you or anybody else in the class using phones?
- How was this impacting you today?

- Exactly right, I want the best for you and your learning, and spending the lesson on your phone is not going to help you do the best you can in this lesson.

Step 3: Plan for restoration and change.

- What was the plan we made when I spoke to you during the lesson and gave you a choice? What did you choose?
- Yes, that's right, if we can't keep our phone on us and use it at the right times, we need to hand them in in the morning. I am going to give your parents a call and just let them know the plan for tomorrow, and then we can try again after that and give you a fresh start to use it appropriately.

Scenario 3: Work refusal

A student in your class who chronically disengages and refuses to work spends an important lesson sitting with their head on the desk. You approached them and they told you that the work was stressing them out, so you gave them a plan to do three questions in the time that was left and that you would speak to them after.

Step 1: Tell our stories, getting curious and checking in.

- Do you know why I wanted to have a chat with you today?
- Yep, that's right, I am really concerned that you aren't doing work and are feeling stressed. Can you explain that to me a little bit more?

Step 2: Explore and acknowledge the harm.

- Thank you for being so open and honest with me about that, I know it's not easy to admit that things are a bit challenging.
- Why do you think we need to get this sorted? Yes exactly, you deserve to learn!

Step 3: Plan for restoration and change.

- What you are describing to me sounds like your upstairs brain and downstairs brain are not talking when you are in the lesson; do you remember me talking about that? I will explain it again.

(Continued)

- Can we think of some strategies for when you are feeling like this to help reconnect your thinking brain?
- That is a great idea to just do some doodling for five minutes when you first come into class! How about the plan is that I set a private timer and let you know when that is up, and you can check in about how you are feeling?

Scenario 4: Inappropriate comments

During a group task you overhear one of the boys saying that he would tell his girlfriend to get into the kitchen and make him a sandwich. After asking him in the lesson whether he understands why that is harmful, it is clear he doesn't, so you said you would discuss it with him after.

Step 1: Tell our stories, getting curious and checking in.

- Are you okay? Do you know why I asked to talk to you during your lunchtime?
- Can you explain what was going on in that lesson and what my concerns might be?
- I'd like to tell you what I saw happening in that lesson and how I was feeling at the time.

Step 2: Explore and acknowledge the harm.

- I would like to explain for you a little bit more what misogyny means and explore that comment that you made.
- After hearing more about it now, why do you think this comment might have been harmful to say?

Step 3: Plan for restoration and change.

- What might we do differently next time? Exactly, not say these things. And why?
- What might you do if somebody else says something like this?
- Thank you, you should be really proud of how well you reflected on this. I am just going to give your mum a call and let her know about this chat.

You might have noticed a few things as I walked through each of those scenarios.

We are talking with the student, not at the student: The nature of the guiding and reflective questions mean that we aren't berating, shaming, or 'giving them a talking to'. We are simply talking with them – a very important distinction if we want our students to be on side for the discussion and work with us to make change.

We don't dictate: If we want our students to take accountability for their behaviours and work with us to resolve them, dictating what they have done wrong, followed by dictating a consequence, is not going to be getting them to truly reflect on what has occurred. They need to come to those conclusions through the discussion and collaborate on a consequence that is fair and makes sense for them. Of course, we can guide them along; however, it should be as student-led as possible.

The consequence isn't always tangible: A student engaging positively in the transformative talk sometimes counts as the consequence itself! It would be superfluous and punitive to give a student an additional consequence for consequence's sake when a resolution has already been reached.

We celebrate their engagement: Don't underestimate how challenging it is for some students to engage positively in the process of one of these talks. Acknowledging that their vulnerability and reflection is a huge accomplishment in itself will support their continued buy-in with your classroom management approach. As a bonus, it also fosters that all-important rapport.

Pillar 3 at a glance

- **The punitive behaviour management strategies that are traditionally used in schools are making things worse, not better.** This is true not only for the students who display the most challenging behaviour, but for us as teachers and the rest of the students in the room.
- **These punitive strategies form the school to prison pipeline.** This is a phenomenon which disproportionately impacts the most vulnerable students, perpetuates systemic racism and causes social exclusion.
- **True discipline is to teach, not to punish.** When we discipline students, we must focus on strategies which encourage reflection, connection, accountability and buy-in.

(Continued)

- **Consequences that create change follow the three Rs.** They must be related to the behaviour, respectful to the student and relevant to the age and context of that student.
- **Providing a consequence is not enough.** We must engage in transformative dialogue to ensure our students have opportunities to grow and develop from the challenges they face. Transformative talks are holistic classroom management in action.

Digging deeper

Listen in:

Hear more about the apology conundrum on Episode 26 of The Unteachables Podcast: *Sorry, Not Sorry: How Apologies Can Be a 'Get Out of Jail Free Card' for Students (and What to Do Instead).*

Add to your bookshelf:

Lost at School: Why Our Kids with Behavioral Challenges are Falling Through the Cracks and How We Can Help Them, Ross W. Greene (Nebraska: Scribner, 2009).

Punished by Rewards: The Trouble with Gold Stars, Incentive Plans, A's, Praise, and Other Bribes, Alfie Kohn (Boston: Houghton Mifflin, 1993).

PILLAR 4
Be Consistent

Students *feeling* safe neurologically and *being* safe physically are vastly different concepts. To teach and reach all students, our classrooms must be islands of safety, places where consistency and predictability rule.

A 'day in the life' …

As you get up out of bed ready to start the day, you feel a deep pit in your stomach. As always, you're due to work at 8am. Whether you get there on time or not is a different story entirely. The train you need to take is often delayed for as long as an hour without any updates, frequently leaving you pacing the platform anxiously awaiting its arrival.

Even when things move like clockwork, you sit on the train unsure of what to expect when you walk through the school gates. Your head of department is notoriously volatile; some days you will be greeted with pleasantries and platters in the staffroom, other days with nit-picking and micromanaging. Will you have the chance to get that presentation for period 4 finished? It isn't a guarantee, as unexpected lesson covers are frequently putting your desperately needed planning periods under threat. At the very least, it'd be good to know you could unpack, make a coffee and get that last-minute copying done. However, much to your chagrin, spur of the moment morning meetings called by your head teacher (the type that could have been an email) are commonplace.

Feeling stressed yet? I'm not surprised.

Although there is plenty of nuance to what constitutes a toxic school environment, one thing is a pretty common factor. A sheer lack of consistency which adds another layer of chaos and challenge to an already challenging job. No matter how you cut it, waking up and dragging yourself into this workplace would be tough. However, if you at least woke up *knowing* how long you'd be waiting for that train, if you *knew* you would at least have time for a morning coffee, you might just be able to head into the day a little more regulated.

Why? Predictability and consistency are the brain's besties.

Let's think about it like this.

You have an attitude-packed chihuahua named Bruce. Every Saturday morning your friend comes over for brunch and a walk. Bruce loves them, wags his little tail frantically in anticipation, bounces up at their legs, eventually rolling onto his back for a nice big belly rub. To Bruce, your friend is familiar and safe.

However, it's a different story when your late-night pizza arrives. Before the unsuspecting delivery driver even knocks on the door, Bruce hears the familiar crunch of gravel under feet on the driveway and starts incessantly barking out the window. Like the good doggo he is, he is simply alerting you to the impending danger that awaits.

You give him a pat, you reassure him, you let him know it was a false alarm and that his human is safe. It is only then that he can calm down. Your pizza gets delivered without a hitch, and nobody gets bitten.

In this scenario, the chihuahua is the amygdala, and the owner is the prefrontal cortex, working together as a team. When things are familiar and predictable, the chihuahua is all licks and pats. However, when potential danger is afoot, there's no time to mess about. He will gnash his teeth and nip at ankles or hide skittishly in the wardrobe with his tail between his legs. That is, until his owner, the prefrontal cortex, comes and reassures him that the threat was a false alarm, or it has got in its car and driven away.

How this applies to our classroom practice

This same concept applies to everything we do in our classrooms. If we, as adults with more developed prefrontal cortexes, are thrown into dysregulation with a high level of inconsistency in our day, then our students whose lives are already fraught with unpredictability are certainly going to be feeling its effects.

It doesn't have to be as extreme as the opening scenario, either. It could simply be students not knowing what is coming up next in a lesson, the time frame they must finish a task, not knowing where they will be sitting, not being sure if they will be able to successfully do the work.

When we increase the level of predictability and consistency in our classrooms, we are creating more familiar friends for their brain's guard dog, the amygdala. We are making it a space with a greater level of felt safety. We are actively supporting the reduction of the stress response in our students and, along with that, proactively nipping challenging classroom behaviours that are a manifestation of the fight, flight or freeze response in the bud.

The 'sciencey' stuff behind it

Embedding strategies which increase the consistency and predictability lesson to lesson are our bread and butter in proactive classroom management. But why is this so impactful?

To understand this, let's take a very quick look at what's happening on a neurological level.

Image 4.1   The brain on uncertainty and predictability

- *It helps students to regulate and anticipate.* The more consistency you can build into your practice, the more achievable self-regulation will be for your students. When students know what to expect, their brains can anticipate and prepare for upcoming events, reducing the activation of the amygdala (involved in fear and emotional responses) and promoting a calmer state. When we anticipate something, our body releases certain chemicals (bio mediators) such as ACTH, cortisol and adrenaline, which help us cope with, and prepare for, the upcoming situation (McEwen and Gianaros, 2010). This consistency also widens the window of tolerance in our students, so they can be more resilient in the face of classroom challenges and demands.

- *It helps students in their executive functioning.* Executive functions (EFs) are mental abilities that allow us to do things such as think, plan, maintain attention and manage unexpected situations. These EFs are impaired by stress; by providing a higher level of consistency within our classrooms, students can develop and strengthen these cognitive processes. This is something that won't just support them with their behaviour, but also with their learning, as it leads to improved self-control and decision-making (Diamond, 2013).

- *It activates the reward pathways in the brain.* Predictability activates the brain's reward pathways. When students know what to expect in the classroom through consistent routines and expectations, their brains release dopamine, a neurotransmitter associated with motivation and pleasure. Put plainly, when students have more consistency in the classroom, they are naturally experiencing their learning in a more enjoyable and rewarding way, the impact of which can be far-reaching for their engagement and behaviour (Berns et al., 2001).

- *Naturally meeting our students' basic needs every lesson.* Let's go back to Pillar 1 when we spoke about William Glasser's Five Basic Needs: the needs which drive behaviour. A higher level of consistency fills a student's survival cup, increasing their felt safety and, in turn, reducing fight, flight or freeze behaviours. Consistency and predictability are also meeting another huge need: the need for power. Power is all about feeling like we can take control and achieve, and with this cup being filled through your consistent pedagogy, our students are less likely to engage in other behaviours that are meeting that need in less than productive ways.

From the above it's easy to see that encasing our classroom spaces in a bubble of predictability is a little bit of proactive classroom management magic.

Putting it into action

School (and life in general) is full of unknowns, for some students more than others. Although we have no control over what happens outside our four walls, there are a multitude of things we *can* do within our practice. Things that make our lessons a place of safety, certainty and, ultimately, of behaviour that is conducive to learning.

The consistency we *can't* control:

- the student in every sense of the word: their behaviour, their context, their struggles and their experiences outside the classroom. Every little unpredictable, inconsistent thing in their lives.

The consistency we *can* control:

- making sure students know exactly what is happening in the lesson, when it's happening and why it's happening;
- differentiating the learning in a way that ensures all students know what success looks like, and how to achieve it, every lesson;
- communicating, modelling and reinforcing our expectations and boundaries explicitly and consistently;
- having routines which guide students to understand what to do at the start of, during and at the end of the lesson;
- our own consistency: our regulation, the relationships we develop, how we welcome them in, how we approach their behaviour.

If you are ever in doubt, here's another easy-to-remember golden rule:

Minimise the unknown.

These things we *can* control? Let's go ahead and package some of them up into a simple and easy to implement toolbox, shall we?

Your consistent classroom toolbox

A predictable start

Do you struggle to gain any semblance of calm at the start of the lesson? Do you have difficulty getting students to engage? Are you dealing with battles from the get-go? In my first few years of teaching my answer was yes, yes and hell yes. This toolbox takes away the guesswork for students at the start of the lesson, helping them swiftly get stuck in without behavioural battles. It is all about how you can increase the predictability for students when they walk into your classroom.

A consistent welcome

Stop and ponder
- Where are you standing when your students walk in?
- Are you welcoming them with a smile?
- Do they know what to expect when they see you?

At the start of this pillar, I spoke about how difficult it is navigating an inconsistent relationship with a boss – how the simple fact of not knowing what kind of person you will get day to day throws you out. To your students, you are that boss. Be the boss that you wouldn't feel anxious waking up to work for every day.

It is important to say at this point that we are human beings and are bound to have a few wobbles from time to time, but do not underestimate the power of being a consistently kind, calm and compassionate figure in a vulnerable young person's life. This can be as simple as focusing on one touch point each lesson. Your welcomes.

Make a commitment to standing at the door and welcoming in each student by name. Names are powerful. When we greet our young people personally it demonstrates a level of effort and care for the individual, it sends a clear message that they are important and that you value them. Every student will benefit from this, but particularly the toughest eggs who are often expecting (and receiving) a far colder reception.

Seating plans

Stop and ponder

- Do your students bounce into the room, pull out any chair and have a seat?
- Does it take them a while to settle where they are, finishing their chats and taking their time unpacking?
- Does where they sit change depending on the day?

A seating plan is a great tangible way to proactively classroom manage. On top of some obvious uses, the one I feel that is most important is not commonly spoken about: the level of predictability and, ultimately, felt safety it provides. When students know where they will be sitting when they walk in, the decision won't be loaded with emotion or anxiety. It takes the guesswork out of it, getting bums on seats quicker, and allows you to crack on with the learning.

Of course, it also allows you to:

- make subtle accommodations for students (e.g. closer to board for students with vision impairment);
- send messages to students that you are calm and in control;
- change up the space if you need to adjust it without it being seen as a punishment (leading to far less protesting from students);
- break up challenging dynamics and reduce low-level behaviours.

Even in contexts where a seating plan may not seem like a behavioural necessity, consider the teaching benefits of getting to know students' names at the start of the year, and having a system that encourages students to move outside their usual bubbles.

The pedagogy around seating plans

You are halfway through the year and haven't got a seating plan? Not a worry, you haven't missed the boat (on the contrary, you're always the one steering it!). When you approach a new seating plan in the right way it can help press the reset button on the class culture and give you a fresh start whenever you choose.

If you're looking to implement (or rejig) a seating plan for your class, follow the steps below. This will allow you to not only get that seating plan sorted, but also do it in a way that will gain that all-important buy-in.

- *Prepare*: At the end of the lesson, give them a heads up that you have worked on a seating plan for the next time they are with you. This way you won't be met with disappointed groans when they arrive the following lesson.
- *Explain*: Explain to your students why you are making this change in a way that is productive and informative rather than punitive. 'I have noticed that there are a few things not working with the way things are, and it is important that I make these changes so when you are in my classroom, you are all learning in the best way you can.'
- *Plan*: The following lesson, it is all systems go! Move forward with your new seating plan from the very start of the lesson. Some ideas on how you can do this calmly are:

  o   put student names on each desk using a piece of tape;
  o   have students wait at the door and call them in calmly one by one;
  o   have the new seating plan projected up on the board as they come in;
  o   keep a copy on your desk so cover teachers can access this for consistency.

Be consistent and be sure to keep this seating plan as an expectation for your students. There is nothing wrong with allowing them to move about into different groups in the lesson; however, making this their starting point will increase the level of predictability, and felt safety, in your space.

Learning maps

Stop and ponder

- When your students walk in the room, is there something they can look at to see what is in store?
- Do your students know what they are learning, and how they are learning it?
- If you asked your students at the end of the lesson if they met the outcomes, would they know what that means?

Learning maps are anything that show students visually what they will be learning that lesson (outcomes) and how they will be getting there (content). This not only makes the lesson itself far more predictable, but, when done consistently, your students will feel a greater sense of ease knowing that in your lesson they won't be caught off guard by that cheeky little group activity.

Why learning maps are an effective consistent classroom management strategy:

- *Reducing anxiety*: When students know exactly what is going to be happening in the lesson, it reduces their stress response and increases their window of tolerance. This is particularly impactful for students who are being led by their stress response. Embedding learning maps every lesson will make students feel increasingly calmer about what they are walking into, in turn reducing disruptive, unsettled and disengaged behaviours.
- *Reinforcing expectations*: You can very clearly demonstrate what you are expecting students to achieve in that lesson and show them *how* you will support them to get there.
- *Making learning visible*: When students see the relevance in their learning, they have more buy-in. When students have more buy-in, we are more likely to see an increase in genuine engagement and a decrease in disengaged behaviours.

The how to:

- Every single lesson *provide an outline of the lesson* for students. This can be something incredibly simple, in student-friendly language. It can be written up, projected up, given to students as a little tick box, it doesn't matter! Just have it there consistently for them.

- Use *simple and student-friendly language*, keep all the really 'teachery' jargon out of it. The last thing we want is for students to be more dysregulated because they are immediately confused by what you're asking from them.
- *Discuss the learning map* after the starter activity; this pedagogy is where the consistency comes in strongly. It means it's not just a superfluous thing sitting there on the board, 'Today we are going to be achieving this (outcome), by doing these tasks (outline)'. This makes the learning for the lesson visible and demonstrates to the students that everything is strategically driven by what they need to know.
- When you are finishing off the lesson, you can *revisit the outcomes* and even use them as the basis of formative tasks, exit slips, questioning strategies as they leave the room. It rounds off the lesson, encourages discussions around learning and, ultimately, keeps students engaged.

Learning maps can be done in a variety of different ways. The example below shows what they can look like and is adapted from Lorraine Munroe's Blackboard Configuration tool. Not only is it quick and easy to implement, but it also supports more rapid lesson planning!

Outcomes	Outline
1. Identify three examples of sensory imagery in poems.	1. Starter activity.
2. Explain the picture that this sensory imagery paints in the reader's mind.	2. Discuss starter activity.
	3. Poem: read as a class and circle the sensory imagery.
	4. Draw it! What comes to mind when you read the poem? Create a visual.
	5. Write it! Explain in your own words how the poet painted a picture with his words.

Starter activites

Stop and ponder

- When your students sit down, what are they doing? Unpacking? Talking? Staring off into the distance?
- Are they waiting for your instruction, or are they 'pens to paper' immediately?
- Do they know exactly where to look and what to do?

Don't you dare underestimate the humble yet mighty starter activity, it is so much more than a quick task or a bit of busy work. Much like many pedagogical strategies, it is far more nuanced and complex than it appears on the surface.

In essence, a starter is a short activity that you provide to students at the very beginning of the lesson. It is designed to conceptually hook students into the learning, and is quick, simple, explicit, timed and achievable.

Why starter activities are consistent classroom management magic:

☐ students come into your lesson knowing that when they sit down, they will be getting a task that is relatable and engaging for them and their lives;
☐ before they walk into the room, they know without a doubt in their mind that they will be successful at something, straight away, no questions asked. This is particularly powerful for the most challenging students who may not feel a great deal of success throughout their day;
☐ as this is a consistent routine, students know to enter the room and start immediately. This mitigates a lot of those disruptive and unsettled low-level behaviours we see when students first enter the room;
☐ it is a non-verbal way of reiterating your expectations to your students and primes them for the learning to come.

But not all starter activities are created equally. For an activity to be impactful, it must meet the following criteria:

• it doesn't rely on any prior knowledge and can stand alone;
• it is academically achievable for every single student in the class;
• it is explicit, timed and clear (three to five minutes);
• it is conceptually related to the lesson outcomes;
• it is relevant to the students themselves to increase buy-in and engagement;
• is projected up/visible on the board/provided to them on paper consistently every lesson.

The following is a very basic example of a starter activity that provides students with an 'in' to the lesson outlined in the learning map: *Brainstorm as many things as you can smell, hear, feel, taste and see right now in the classroom in the next three minutes.*

Consistent non-verbals

Imagine being able to create an unspoken language with your students? One where they just know what you expect of them moment to moment without needing to say a word? Well, this little bit of classroom management magic exists, and it's all in the strategic use of your non-verbals!

Stop and ponder

- When you require attention from your class, are you aware of how and where you are standing?
- Are you modelling the stillness and quiet you want back from each student?
- Are you a living, breathing representation of your expectations?

One of the biggest challenges teachers have with classroom management is waiting for the class's attention. You know the drill: you stand and you wait, say 'It's your time you're wasting not mine', and wait some more. Meanwhile, there are seemingly inextinguishable pockets of spot-fires burning away. When it comes to this frustrating dilemma, your spots matter a lot and, by hardwiring 'attention spots' (a concept by Michael Grinder's ENVoY) into your pedagogy, your position can calmly signal to your students that you are ready for them to listen, talk, learn and chat.

When you want to capture the attention of the class at any point during the lesson, consistently follow these steps.

1. *Choose a specific spot* in your classroom that will serve as your attention spot. It is best that it is front and centre!
2. *Be consistent with this spot* and use it every single time you require the class's attention (this will eventually become a powerful hardwired visual signal).
3. *Deploy a simple and short call to attention*, 'Okay Year 8, back to the big group in five, four, three …' with a non-verbal hand signal, such as a hand up.
4. *Tune in to your body language.* How are you carrying yourself? Are you standing solidly on both feet, credibly, up straight? Are you slouching? Are you confident or are you sending the opposite message? What is your teaching presence when you are in this space?
5. *Remain calm and composed and wait.* Don't keep calling out, don't keep raising your voice above the noise, refrain from any complicated requests, just wait. This stage can be challenging, but remain confident. With repetition, it will become quicker and more effective.
6. *Uphold high expectations of attention*; near enough is not good enough, as small spot-fires will yet again turn to bushfires. It is crucial for every student to listen attentively. By teaching over the chatter, you inadvertently convey a non-verbal message that their engagement is unimportant and it undermines the boundaries you've set.

7. *Repeat your call to attention* if things are still chaotic and loud. However, be mindful of how and when you do this. Too often, and you'll just be adding to the noise and detracting from your non-verbal communication.

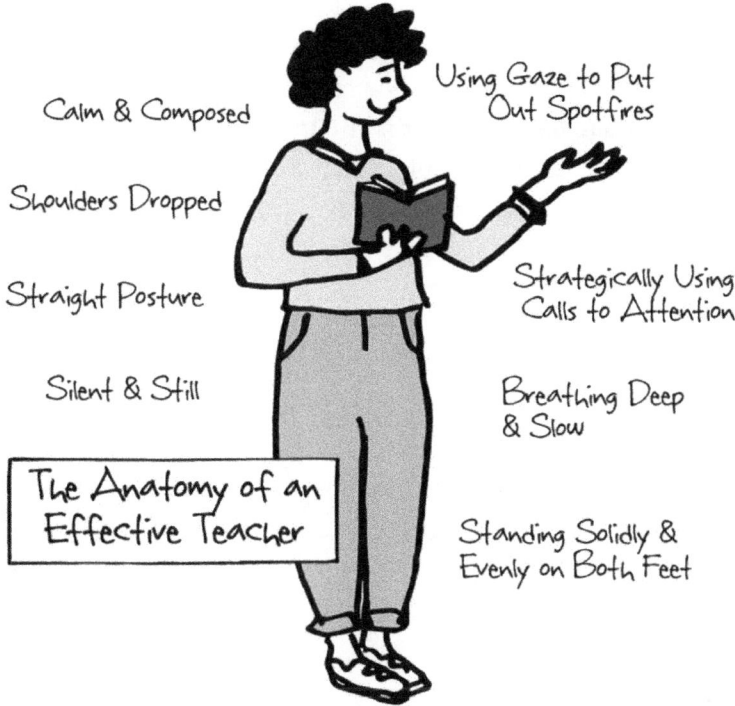

Image 4.2   The anatomy of a teacher effectively waiting for attention

There is often a concern that spending a significant amount of time waiting for attention can result in unnecessarily wasted learning time. However, it's important to remember that if you don't have the class's attention, it won't be productive either way. See this strategy as a long-term investment! Over time, as you transition from a group activity to the attention spot, you'll notice students naturally preparing themselves to listen attentively to what comes next.

Pillar 4 at a glance

- **Consistency and predictability are the brain's best friend.** They help to reduce the stress response and regulate, support executive functioning, help students meet their basic needs and activate the reward pathways in the brain.

(Continued)

- **Increasing consistency and predictability in classroom practice supports proactive classroom management.** It reduces the stress response, reducing those dysregulated behaviours, as well as communicating expectations clearly and explicitly.
- **Whenever in doubt, follow the rule of thumb: 'minimise the unknown'.** You can do this in your classroom space by using strategies such as a consistent welcome, seating plans, starter activities, learning maps and non-verbal cues.
- **It's not just about behaviour, it's about the learning!** These pedagogies not only foster a positive classroom culture, but a productive learning culture where all students can engage and feel success from the moment they walk in the room.

Digging deeper

Listen in:

Let me guide you through the why and the how of seating plans on Episode 35 of The Unteachables Podcast: *Increasing Felt Safety (and Reducing Challenging Behaviours) Through Consistency and Predictability. A Deep Dive into the Humble Seating Plan.*

Add to your bookshelf:

The Teacher and the Teenage Brain: Understanding Adolescent Development, Teaching and Learning, John Coleman (London: Routledge, 2021).

The Developing Mind, Dan Siegel (New York: Guilford Press, 1999).

PILLAR 5
Be Clear

One of the biggest gifts we can give to our students is to always assume they are doing the very best they can, with the information and knowledge that they have at the time.

Free fruit!

First period every Friday morning, my rambunctious Year 8 class would bound into the room, chugging cans of electric green energy drink and hangrily snacking on sour gummy strips. Instead of being 'that nagging teacher', reciting the A–Z of why taurine and sugar did not constitute a balanced breakfast, I had a bright idea.

I would create a 'sustenance station' on my desk: a bowl of fresh fruit to offer the students as they came in. Feeling excited and inspired I got to work immediately; the very next morning, I was lugging a big bag of produce up to my classroom and filling up a bowl adorned with a sign, 'Take one! – Miss English'. I looked at it proudly and awaited their arrival.

So, let's first talk about my 'quality world' expectations here. A few students bashfully approaching, 'Miss English, can I please take a banana?', slinking away and eating it quietly at their desk while getting on with their work. Having them wave a jolly goodbye at the end of the lesson to their teacher who cared enough to get them something to eat. You see where I am going with this? I know, you don't have to tell me, I have no idea how I didn't see it coming.

The reality? Cue the carnage. As quickly as I pointed to the bowl, every single student thronged to my desk. It was a walking-dead-style swarm, with hands and arms reaching from within the hoard of teenage bodies that surrounded me at all angles. They clambered desperately over one another; pieces of fruit flying out of the bowl at time-lapse speed. It took less than a minute for the great fruit battle of 2012 to come to its bloody conclusion, leaving in its wake a shroud of apple cores, banana skins and orange peels. A lucky few making it all the way to the outskirts of the fruity basketball hoop bin. The students who were casualties in the battle of fruit, unable to secure a morsel, were now vocalising their disappointment, hunger and despair. Some swearing, some slumping and some simply choosing to leave.

The inaugural, and the final, free fruit sustenance station, had come to a devastating end, leaving a deflated Miss English spending the remaining 60 minutes of the lesson attempting to regain any semblance of control.

These impulsive, energetic, forever hungry Year 8 students saw it and, of course, went for it; can you blame them? Oh yes, blame them I did.

But what had happened? I was expecting my students to do something that I hadn't explained. Something I hadn't been clear about. I might as well have tipped a bunch of fruit on the floor and squished it deep into the carpet myself.

Why? This brings me onto the next golden rule:

If you expect it, you must explain it.

When I talk about explaining, I don't mean just giving it a verbal once over. Most of the time it takes far more than that, which is true of everything we do in our classroom space. We make so many assumptions on the daily. We assume our students know where the boundaries are, what to do with the work, how to enter the room in a way we want them to, how to leave the room, how to get themselves into groups, how to contribute to tasks … the list is endless.

Yet what is often happening is we are expecting things we don't explicitly explain, leaving ourselves open to a fruit free-for-all.

A big part of proactive classroom management is our ability to be as clear and explicit as we possibly can with our students on the what, the why and the how of everything in our lessons. And I mean everything.

Stop and ponder

How often have you sat down and actually *completed* a task that you have created for your students?

This is called living the lesson, and it is a surefire way to locate any gaps, predict any misconceptions and get an accurate gauge on what works and what doesn't. Those things we think we have been clear on? Well, it might just surprise us to know that, when it comes to crunch time, it doesn't quite translate in the same way.

Try it: next time you create a task for your class, spend five minutes with everything in front of you and give it a run through. See what pops up, where you get stuck, how long it takes, whether or not the prompts are adequate. If you find anything sticky, your students certainly will.

Now, when I look back and consider what it truly means to be the teacher I needed, it wasn't about fruit or anything of the like. It wasn't about my personality or ego, nor was it about things that would warrant a please or a thank you. It was about always assuming the best of my students, rather than thinking they were purposefully non-compliant or simply not engaging. It was about providing them with the clarity they needed to know better and do better, both behaviourally and academically.

It was my teaching practice. The things that they would never be able to pinpoint as me being the teacher they needed but feeling it through safety, security and success every single time they walked into my classroom.

What do I mean by clarity?

Fendick explains clarity in our classroom practice as having four dimensions:

1. *Clarity of organisation*: The way we structure the lesson, how we state objectives clearly and review these at the end of the lesson.
2. *Clarity of explanation*: How we communicate what we are trying to get the students to do in the lesson, behaviourally and academically.
3. *Clarity of examples and guided practice*: How we are clearly communicating expectations to students and how we support them to reach these expectations. Again, this relates to things that are both academic and behavioural.
4. *Clarity of assessment of student learning*: How visible the learning is, and how both teacher and student understand whether progress and learning has taken place.

At the very centre of these four things is the way we, as the teacher, can communicate with our students verbally and non-verbally (Fendick, 1990).

Clarity is so crucial in our teaching practice that it ranked number 24 out of 252 influences related to student achievement in John Hattie's study *Visible Learning* (2008). To put it into perspective, teacher humour ranked 230 (luckily for me), teacher subject matter knowledge ranked 213 and reducing class sizes, which a lot of teachers see as being a potential holy grail solution of classroom management woes, ranked 186.

But wait, isn't this a classroom management book? You're sounding very 'teaching and learning-ish'. Remember that this book is called *It's Never Just About the Behaviour*, and teaching and learning is a huge piece of the classroom management puzzle. When we increase the clarity in our lessons, we are simultaneously increasing a student's ability to find enjoyment in learning and academically achieve (Chen and Lu, 2022).

Your clear classroom toolbox

When we aren't expecting our students to play a guessing game, when we can communicate clearly and precisely what we want from them at any given time, we foster classroom cultures of trust, rapport and regulation. Challenging behaviours rarely thrive under these conditions. Yet as the four dimensions of clarity of practice highlight, there is quite a bit more to it than explaining things clearly to students (although this certainly helps).

The following toolbox will provide you with explicit strategies to communicate your expectations to students both academically and behaviourally. You simply can't separate the two!

Clear expectations

I once believed I needed to start the year off strong, with a strong persona to match. Rules were set to ensure that there were as few disruptions as possible: don't talk when others are talking; don't get out of your seats and run around without permission; don't get up and walk out of the room; don't chew gum; don't eat in class; don't slap each other across the back of the head. You agree? Yes? You must; you have no option. Sign this agreement so it's set in stone. Done and dusted!

Then what would happen? Students would talk when others are talking. Students got out of their seats and ran around, munching on chippies and chewy. Students walked in and out of the room when they were facing an inevitable 'Year 9-style' friendship crisis. Of course, it happened. A few expectations aren't going to stop the floodgates from opening!

Let's think about the reason we set expectations in the first place, shall we?

- So students can understand *how* to behave in our classrooms.
- So students can *buy in* to our classroom management approach.
- So students know what to do to *make things right* when things go wrong.

If these are the reasons, setting rules in a traditional sense can never reach these goals.

The problem

What is wrong with this style of rule setting? They are an out-of-context, arbitrary list of not-to-dos, with zero relevance or buy-in and, most importantly, they aren't providing the clarity that students need to be able to behave in ways that are more positive in a classroom context.

These black and white rules? Don't quite account for you slipping your muesli bar to a student who didn't get time for breakfast because they are caring for their siblings. Or the student who got out of their seat to grab a pre-arranged fidget toy. Unless you want an entire class up in arms over the sheer lack of equality, you need to approach it differently.

This is before we even touch on the fact that delivering rules in this way is fracturing relationships and escalating low-level behaviours before you even begin. It is placing shame and fear, the kings of disconnection, at the very core of your classroom management approach.

The solution

There are so many things left out in the murky unknown when we approach expectations in this way. What happens when these expectations aren't met? What are students supposed to do instead? How is this reflected in the day-to-day approach to classroom management? How does this reflect and take into consideration the hundreds, if not thousands of nuances with the behaviours you're putting a big red cross through?

So how do we do this in a way that is not only going to be clearer for our students, but gain that all-important buy-in when needed? Well let's think about this in a couple of ways.

Do students even understand what expectations are and why they are important?

Let's be honest with ourselves for a moment. Our students probably aren't going to care a whole lot about the rules we dictate to them at the start of the year — especially the students who are most likely to struggle with them. Why should they care about them? What are expectations anyway? Aren't you just trying to control me, teacher!?

Students need to feel connected to their learning, whether it's an English lesson, or a lesson on expectations. A good way to do this to make it real-world relevant for them and follow my three Ws of concept-based teaching.

Applying the three Ws of concept-based teaching to a lesson on expectations:

- *What?* What are expectations? Does the concept of expectations make sense to your students? Bust any misconceptions and be clear about what they are.
- *Where?* Where do students see expectations in their real world? Do they have expectations around screen time, bedtime, mealtime, sports, other extra-curricular activities?
- *Why?* Why are expectations important? Why do they exist at home and in other parts of their lives? Why might these be extended to a classroom context? What might the purpose and importance of these be (for both us as teachers and them as students).

Image 5.1   The three Ws of teaching a new concept

Are students involved in the process of expectation setting?

If we want greater buy-in, our students need to come along on the journey. Human beings simply don't thrive in systems wherein they are dictated to; this is true of us as adults and our students.

Being a proactive and engaged participant in setting these expectations rather than a passive receiver of them meets their basic psychological need for autonomy, competence and relatedness, as described in self-determination theory (Ryan and Deci, 2000). This level of student voice and participation is also linked to improved academic achievement, increased self confidence and more positive attitudes towards school in general (Fielding, 2004). Fielding explores the notion of speaking 'with' our students rather than 'for' them, a concept that fosters greater inclusion and empowerment within our classroom communities.

Yet, we need to be clear about how students can be involved in the process. Remember, whatever we expect, we must explain. Going back to the four dimensions of clarity, if we are expecting students to contribute to their expectations, we need to provide them with the explicit support needed to do so.

What this looks like when you are setting expectations:

- *Asking strategic questions*: Strategic questioning will allow your students to carefully consider the answers they will contribute to the discussion to have their ideas and voices heard. These types of questions can be verbally asked, or presented as prompts or sentence starters.

  'What do you think students need to do at school and why?'

  'What do you think is fair for me to expect of you as a student?'

  'What makes the class feel nice and calm?'

- *All voices heard*: It is crucial we are creating authentic opportunities for all students to contribute their ideas. This will look different from individual to individual, so can be done in a variety of ways including (but not limited to):
  - *verbal* contributions through class and peer discussion
  - *non-verbally* through sticky notes
  - *voting* on the expectations they think are fair and equitable.

The important thing is having each student contribute to the process in some way to ensure a higher level of buy-in to the expectations throughout the year.

- *All in agreement*: Once we have our expectations somewhat decided upon, we should be providing opportunities to openly discuss any concerns or disagreements students have with them. This will give you the chance to talk through any misconceptions, justify their importance, or reframe them to make them more relatable and fairer for your class.

  'I am going to give ten minutes to read over these expectations we have voted on.'

  'Are there any that you don't think are fair or necessary?'

  'Are there any that don't make sense?'

Remember, these expectations will be absolutely superfluous if you don't have your class on board. Spending the time working through this with them clearly and explicitly will pay dividends down the track.

Are your expectations a values system, or just punitive rules in disguise?

Rules are rules. Black and white. No wiggle room. They may be equal, but they are not equitable, and we are working with students with incredibly diverse and nuanced contexts.

What you want for expectations are the opposite of this. When done right, they should be a core values system for your class that you can continue to return to time after time after time again.

If you tend to lean on the more 'rules' route, consider how you can reframe these.

- 'No talking when others are talking,' turns into, 'We listen to and respect the voices and opinions of others.'
- 'I must complete all set work,' is flipped to, 'We do the best work we can.'
- 'We are in class on the bell,' becomes, 'We respect the lesson start and finish times.'

These seemingly subtle changes are saying very similar things; however, they allow our students the grace and flexibility to be the human beings that they are. Sometimes they will be late, sometimes they won't be able to complete a task despite their best efforts, sometimes they will need to interrupt you to go to the toilet before they do something far worse at their desk.

How are you modelling these, using these, being a living, breathing, representation of these?

If you hit all the above and develop a clear set of expectations that act as a beautiful collaborative values system for your class, you're not done yet. Wait, what? Yep. This is only half of it. Unless we authentically weave them into our classroom management approach, they will get lost in the ether (almost immediately, let's be honest).

I don't mean popping them up on the wall and forgetting about them, either. If anything, taking this approach will just be a constant reminder to all of you of how much of a waste of time that lesson was if there will be no follow-up. They need to be visible, frequently referenced, utilised in our transformative talks, modelled.

How might this look in practice?

A student decides to come into the classroom late disrupting the learning of others.

You have a transformative talk with them where you can use questioning strategies that get them to reflect on the expectations that you have of them in the classroom.

- 'Have a look back at the expectations we set as a class, are there any that we might have struggled with today?'

- 'Can I suggest what you might have had a bit of difficulty with?'
- 'Can you remember when we spoke about this and why it was important?'
- 'How might we work towards meeting this expectation in the following lesson?'

You are running late to class and have a coffee in your hand.
You're feeling frazzled and arrive to your whole class waiting outside the classroom. You get them inside the room and settled and you model taking accountability for not meeting expectations.

- 'Today I didn't meet the expectation of respecting our class time. I wasn't prepared and on time. Remember it's never an excuse but it explains it, I had a really tough morning.'
- 'I am sorry that you were waiting outside.'
- 'I always try to make sure this doesn't happen; I am human, and I have hard days like we all do.'

Clear task instructions: What are we doing?

I know the struggle, what teacher doesn't? You spend a chunk of time explaining a task in detail, what to do, when to do it, how to do it. You finally send students off to crack on with what needs to be done.

Cue the blank faces.

Cue the side-eye glances.

Cue the … 'Miss, what are we doing?'

Cue the brain explosion of 'I just freaking told you!'

First, let's just cut these kids some slack. How often have you had to rewind a TV programme, re-read a page in a book, or ask somebody to repeat themselves? We are all human beings who struggle to process things and maintain focus and attention, even when it is something we are interested in!

The problem

You are one person trying to relay information to 30 different students. If you were able to verbally communicate to every single one of them exactly what to do with a task, the first time you explain it, it would be a feat of miraculous proportions.

Very often verbal instructions are missed. This is not because a student was being naughty, purposely non-compliant, or not respecting what you're up there saying. It really is just that hard to keep that level of attention when somebody is talking!

This is true of neurotypical students, but even more so with neurodiverse students and those with other additional needs. For so many students, understanding and following multi-step instructions is just an unnecessary challenge that we can very easily put strategies in place to overcome.

The solutions

Go visual.

Ask yourself: If I lost my voice right now, how would I best communicate this to the class?

The goal is to limit the amount of teacher talk used. Why? How long can *you* sit there and listen to a colleague talk about a topic that you aren't 100 per cent passionate about before your attention starts to wane? When we increase the visuals we use with our class, we increase the level of visual support that our students can access. This then decreases the amount of time we need to repeat ourselves, as we have a tool at our disposal to provide, point to, or project up.

Rather than explaining things verbally which you will then need to waste time re-explaining to a number of students, have your instructions written up as a step-by-step, a check-box task card, a to do list, or any other way that you want to present what students need to do.

Whatever way you choose doesn't matter, it just needs to be explicit, clear, concise and written in student-friendly language.

Success criteria

A success criterion is a succinct breakdown of what students need to do, or include, in order to complete a task or meet an outcome successfully. It is written in language that students understand (so stay away from any complex curriculum jargon) and is a tool for students to be able to get really clear on what they need to do to be successful.

What it looks like

Imagine students need to write a report on bees. In order to get really clear on what students need to do in order for them to complete that task successfully, you provide them with a success criterion which says:

I have:

☐   written a catchy title;
☐   included four body paragraphs on different ideas about bees;

☐   followed the point, example, explanation (PEE) structure;
☐   referenced four different websites;
☐   written in third person;
☐   used four different literary devices;
☐   included a bibliography.

You can provide these to students prior to the task, ensuring that you are clear in your explanation of them by going through each point and busting any misconceptions.

Better yet, try writing them collaboratively! Guide the conversation with some strategic questions while jotting down their ideas on the board. This will help you to create your success criteria, while simultaneously making the learning more visible and increasing understanding around the talk.

Examples of questions you might ask:

•   'What does a quality report need?'
•   'When we write our paragraphs, what do we do?'
•   'How do we start a report?'
•   'How do we make our reports really interesting?'
•   'How do we make sure our reports are factual?'

Timers

How much time do your students have to *think* about the task or *invest* in the class?

How can they know if they are *rushing* it, or taking too long?

How much *detail* are they supposed to be putting into it?

Tasks that have an explicit time attached provide the level of clarity that students need in order to tackle things in the best way possible. Remember that we can't expect what we don't explain, and if we aren't explicit about the details of tasks such as timings, we can't get ourselves in a bother when they write one sentence, pop their pens down and say, 'Done!' Providing visible timers also supports them to stay on task, minimising low-level behaviours and producing a higher quality of work.

Being clear on the language around timed tasks also matters:

•   'You have 15 minutes for this task, so if you finish earlier look back to your success criteria to see if you need to add anything in.'
•   'Have a look up on the board; five minutes remaining.'

- 'Everyone looks like they are still working hard on this, so I am going to add another three minutes to the timer.'

Why are these effective tools?

As teaching and learning tools all the above enable students to complete tasks and meet outcomes in a more meaningful way, as well as embedding strategies that make learning visible for students. When learning is more visible and students are able to understand the *why* behind that *what*, there is an increased level of buy-in and engagement to what you are teaching them.

As a classroom management tool this level of clarity takes the guesswork out of tasks and, as students know exactly what you're expecting and what success looks like, it provides the safety and security needed for them to engage in their learning. As students feel increasingly capable, confident and supported, there will naturally be a decrease in disengagement and challenging low-level behaviours.

Clear verbal instructions: Go!

Think about the last time you told your class to clean up at the end of the lesson, or get themselves into groups of three for an activity, or get started on a task, or anything else you've expected them to do. Does your class nail it every time? Are there some stragglers?

The problem

Precisely the same problem as when we try to give students verbal instructions for a task. They can very easily become lost (at no fault of ours or the students). It is in the territory of being a human being and not automatically being able to process and understand every bit of data that comes our way.

The solution

Get ready, get set, GO!

Whether you're providing verbal instructions or visual instructions (a mixture of both is always a winner when appropriate), *follow the get ready, get set and go strategy.*

Image 5.2 *Get ready, get set, go!*

What this sounds like

Example 1

Instead of 'Okay everybody, the bell is going to go soon, let's clean up!', let's think about the end of the lesson. The bell goes and students run out. Behind them, the usual classroom clutter. Chewed up pen lids, pieces of paper, chairs untucked, drawn-on tables askew. The last thing you have time to do is go around and straighten everything up. Yet a clear classroom space is crucial for a calm class to follow, so you go about the work of clean-up.

If this sounds like something you're experiencing, then you're not alone. Yet it is certainly something to get on top of, and here is how you do it.

Try:

Get ready: Okay Year 8, attention up the front! *Practise the pause* We have five minutes left of the lesson so we are going to be packing up.

Get set: I would like you all to return to your desks, pack up all of your things, pick up any rubbish on the floor around you and be standing behind your desks within four minutes. I will be choosing which tables/desks go first!

Go: Okay, the timer is up on the board; let's go! (You'll notice I use timers in all these verbal instructions, too – again, increasing how explicit and clear the expectations are. No excuses!) When the time is up: 'Wonderful job, Temi's row; you can head off first. Hmm, looks like Ali's group is ready too, excellent! Have a lovely lunch!'

Example 2

Instead of *'Move* back into the groups you were in last lesson!', try the following.

Get ready: You will be shortly moving back into the same groups as you were in last lesson.

Get set: For this you are going to be going back to the same places you were in, bringing only your writing books and pens, and be sitting down ready for my instructions in three minutes.

Go: Are there any questions on what you were doing last lesson? Okay, you can move into your groups now. Three minutes up on the board!

Example 3

Instead of 'Okay everybody, head on into the library now and grab a seat!', try the following.

Get ready: We are going to be heading on into the library now so we can do some research on the computers.

Get set: You are going to be going straight in and sitting on the floor in front of the whiteboard so I can give you your instructions for the task. Remember that when we are in the library, we need to use our private voices.

Go: Head on in now Year 7. Great job, Henry. Brilliant work getting ready, Jamil!

Clear verbal instructions: Stop!

Stop running! Don't chuck that paper across the room! Stop talking! Stop this, stop that. Don't do this, don't do that. My day would be riddled with it. However, telling students to simply stop doing something does not provide the clarity that is needed for our students to successfully meet those expectations.

Stop and ponder

Before going down the route of stopping the behaviour, look through your critical and reflective lens to consider why it is important or necessary for the behaviour to be stopped in the first place. Sit up straight! Look me in the eyes. Sit still! Stop fidgeting. Behaviours such as these are traditionally seen as non-compliance, but are in fact neurologically, biologically or developmentally normal and expected.

So, when it comes to these behaviours, stop and ponder.

What is the purpose? If children can't stop fidgeting, moving, or talking, why might that be?

What accommodations can be made? How can you explicitly plan for more of this in your lesson?

The problem

When we tell students to stop doing something, there is the potential for students to have a lack of understanding around what the expectation is.

Why should they stop that?

What should they do instead?

As mentioned in previous pillars, true discipline means to teach. The same issue is bound to pop up again. If we tell students to stop doing something without being clear on alternatives, we are missing vital opportunities to build their skills when it does.

The solution

Let's start by flipping our thinking. Instead of jumping to a response born from frustration and automatically assuming non-compliance, get curious about why the student may be behaving in that way. Are they unsure of the alternative? Are they just testing the waters with you? Are they looking for a reaction? Are they just blissfully unaware of the expectations?

Then move on to flipping our approach. There are several ways that we can break the cycle of the don'ts and stops.

1. *Flip it! Idea 1*: State the expected behaviour.

   Instead of: Stop running around the building Temi!

   Try: We walk when we are in the building, thank you Temi!

   Why: Flipping this language reiterates the expectations to your students while still addressing the behaviour and giving them a direct instruction. It acts as a reminder, rather than an order, which in most circumstances works to resolve the issue in a supportive way.

2. *Flip it! Idea 2*: Lead with thank you, rather than please.

   Instead of: Please stop running around the building Temi!

   Try: We walk when we are in the building, thank you Temi!

   Why: A pre-emptive 'thank you' sends a message to the student that you are already expecting the request to be fulfilled.

3. *Flip it! Idea 3*: Let your visuals do the talking.

   Instead of: Stop calling out; or Don't call out your answers.

   Try: Having visual reminders up next to your teaching points for anything you feel like you are always repeating.

   Why: You can just point to the visual reminder each time you need to say it. It acts as a constant reminder for students, and having this up in a visible space will begin to hardwire this instruction for students. When you create a visual prompt, you are also avoiding a head to head; the behaviour being corrected is then about the expectation, the visual on the wall, not about you vs them.

4. *Flip it! Idea 4*: Put the ball in their court.

   Instead of: Stop calling out!

   Try: Temi, do you see your classmates waiting patiently with their hands up? (in private voice)

   Why: Turning your request into a question may support students to reflect on their behaviours, in turn raising their accountability and empathy. Getting them thinking also gives you much more of a chance of reducing that behaviour over time as they will begin to understand the reason and buy into this change.

Pillar 5 at a glance

- Follow the golden rule: **If you expect it, you must explain it.**
- **Avoid assuming purposeful non-compliance.** When students are not following instructions or meeting expectations, we need to stop, think and reflect. Was this because they were choosing not to comply, or was this because I wasn't clear on what to do and how to do it?
- **Expectations are not just a lesson, they are a culture.** A start of the year lesson doesn't cut it to set our students up for success when it comes to expectations around learning and behaviour. We need to make these a values system in our classrooms that we can return to time and time again.
- **Giving students instructions for a task requires more than some verbal steps.** Go visual as much as possible through task cards, checklists and written steps in order to decrease task confusion, save your voice and give your students (and yourself) the best chance of a successful lesson.
- **When giving students verbal instructions, follow the get ready, get set, go method**. This will increase the clarity you are providing and, along with it, your chances of getting students to successfully follow them.
- **Saying 'stop' is not a clear request.** We can better support students to make alternative choices by reframing our directions. State the expected behaviour, use strategic questions, use visuals and pre-emptively thank students.

Digging deeper

Listen in:

Want a verbal step-by-step on expectation setting? Listen in to Episode 35 of The Unteachables Podcast: *A Step-by-Step Guide on How to Set Expectations, and (More Importantly) Make Them an Effective Part of Your Day-to-Day Classroom Management.*

Add to your bookshelf:

When the Adults Change, Everything Changes: Seismic Shifts in School Behaviour, Paul Dix (Bancyfelin, Carmarthen: Independent Thinking Press, 2017).

Minding Bodies: How Physical Space, Sensation, and Movement Affect Learning (Teaching and Learning in Higher Education), Susan Hrach (Morgantown: West Virginia University Press, 2021).

The Inclusive Classroom: A New Approach to Differentiation, Daniel Sobel (London: Bloomsbury, 2021).

PILLAR 6
Be Challenging

Fiercely believing that a child can achieve is a powerful act of compassion. Giving them the right support and insisting that they do so? Well, that right there is life changing.

Introduction

In primary school I was textbook studious. My hand was always the first to shoot up. I was the first in line, and the last to leave the lesson. My exercise book was adorned with meticulously ruled pages, underlined titles, green ticks and 'Great work!' scratch and sniff stickers. I still recall beaming with pride when my Year 5 teacher told me that I could be anything that I wanted to be.

I believed them. The bar was set high.

Until suddenly I was no longer that girl. By the time I reached Year 8, things in my household took a turn. Severe mental illness had its grip tight around my mum and, as the only other girl in the house, my dad set his sights on me as the homemaker. I was a child turned carer, counsellor, maid and mediator. I went from a little girl full of promise, to the glue (barely, and silently) holding together a family in crisis.

The light in me faded, as did the connection I felt with everybody around me. I was alien, heavy with responsibility and loss, second to sadness and sickness; confused by the debilitating illness that had taken the mother that I knew; angry, saddened and resentful at my father for reasons that were beyond a young girl's comprehension.

Of course, this isn't what my teachers saw – because, as a result of these things, I was angry, defiant and provocative. I spent my lessons making snide remarks, yelling out and wearing my newfound personality as a mask. Classwork? Minimal. The little work I did complete was on a torn-out piece of paper, then shoved in the bottom of my bag or crumpled up and thrown in the bin on the way out. Homework and assignments? Forget about it.

The girl with the world at her feet was gone, replaced by a teenager who was told by teachers, her parents, her year advisors, that 'School isn't your thing; do a trade, get a job.' A clever ruse to just move me out of school, and out of their hair. Eventually, my teachers stopped caring if I completed my work, brought a pen, or even showed up to class. I was a ghost.

The bar was lowered.

They no longer believed in me, and I no longer believed in myself. 'They are right,' I thought, 'I don't belong here.'

Despite this, the fear of the world unknown had me clinging onto school until my final years. This, I'm sure, was much to the dismay of my teachers who looked at their 2007 class list and saw my name. All but one.

Miss Povey was your typical English teacher; she lived and breathed literature, always at her desk, glasses lowered, with an annotated classic in her hand. English came quite easily to me, so naturally my subject choices for the final two years of school consisted of everything English, all taught by poor Miss Povey. She sniffed my affinity for the subject out a mile away and, all of a sudden, I had a teacher who didn't care that I wore my skirt too short or my eyeliner too thick. She didn't care that I reeked of cigarettes, and she ignored the earphone poorly concealed beneath my scarf. She cared that I was in that class; she cared that I did English.

The bar was raised.

In fact, Miss Povey raised that bar so high for me that I didn't think it was possible to reach it. Homework, essays, pages and pages of writing, readings to be completed and annotated. Most times I failed, sometimes I succeeded, yet her belief never waned. For the first time in six years, I had green marks in my book, a paragraph in a creative writing piece adorned with the words 'This part here, this is genius'. That moment changed my life, and I wish she knew that.

When I got right to the finish line and my confidence faltered, I told her I wasn't going to show up for the final High School Certificate exams. In her dry and no bull fashion, she simply said two words. Band six. Band six, the highest possible grade.

And band six is what I got.

Not only did I finish high school, but I was invited back to the awards ceremony for high achievers where I accepted awards in front of a throng of teachers. Teachers who didn't believe it was possible for me. And Miss Povey, watching on, as if it were no big deal.

This brings me onto my next golden rule of holistic classroom management.

> If you set the bar low, that is exactly where they will go.

Our students will rise to (or fall to) the bar we set for them. Which is why when it comes to an approach that is genuinely proactive in mitigating and addressing classroom behaviour, the way we approach student learning and achievement is paramount.

What a low bar looks like

In the name of total transparency and solidarity, when I first became a teacher, oh boy did I lower that bar for some of my students. Even with my own demoralising experiences of school, when faced with a class full of 'mini me's (and students with far greater needs), I did whatever I could to survive.

See, when you're trying to keep your head above water in a class full of challenging students, expectations slip, you pick your battles and you do what works. And guess what works to gain back some semblance of control and compliance? Crosswords, copying, colouring and basic comprehension. All of the things that are the antithesis of challenge.

I'd plan lessons designed to get students composing, creating, analysing and debating, all of those brilliant things any English teacher would want from a quality lesson. Yet it wouldn't be long before my good intentions were pushed against and overthrown. I went down the path of least resistance. Throwing in the towel, turning a blind eye and writing notes on the board for students to copy. They would comply, as if a switch was flicked, and peacefully spend the remainder of the lesson copying chunks of writing into their books or resting their heads on their desks. A happy trade-off for a desperate teacher.

If you too have fallen into this trap, you are not alone. In fact, it is so common that there's even a name for it: the *pedagogy of poverty*.

The pedagogy of poverty

Upon conducting research in schools around the US, Martin Haberman, a professor of curriculum and instruction, identified some stark teaching trends for which he coined this name. He observed that in schools with greater concerns around attainment, attendance and behaviour, students were being given 'busy work' rather than being taught in a way that helped them to think critically, get engaged and succeed in their learning (Haberman, 2010). The goal? Keep them quiet and keep them compliant.

The types of strategies that dominate in the pedagogy of poverty are those I naturally fell back on, as do so many others, as we are scrambling to survive. The strategies that keep the bar low. Little output, little expectation for progress, very little stretch and very little challenge.

Why this works

Instead of teaching and learning practices being a powerful pathway to academic attainment, with the pedagogy of poverty, low-order thinking and low-level expectations are a tool to increase control and compliance. Let's talk about why this works.

As you know from previous pillars, a lot of the challenging behaviours that we see in our classroom can be attributed to dysregulation. When the amygdala signals that a threat is present, it starts the hormonal cascade to remove that threat and keep us safe through fight, flight, or freeze.

This is the first way that teaching and learning is inextricably linked with behaviour. When students enter a classroom and are given work that they don't feel capable or confident to complete, their brains can register this as a threat. They will then push back on this challenge; they will fight against us, flee from the room, or freeze and disengage entirely. If we then take away the requirement of challenge or stretch, we too take away the threat and biologically reduce those fight, flight or freeze behaviours. They thank you, by happily and quietly making their way through a worksheet, a cloze passage, or copying down definitions.

It really does work! Classroom management success! Well, that is, if the goal is to simply manage challenging behaviours. As teachers we need to manage behaviours so our students can learn, not manage the learning so our students can behave.

A self-fulfilling prophecy

Keeping the bar low has a far more insidious impact than simply controlling classroom behaviour lesson to lesson. Yes, we are physically limiting their academic potential through the lack of stretch or challenge. However, what is truly concerning with this approach is the messages we are sending our students about what we expect of them, what we believe about them, and what we think they are capable of.

When we keep the bar low, the types of things our students might be *hearing* from us are:

- I don't care if you complete your work;
- I don't care if you are disengaged;
- you won't be successful anyway;
- you aren't worth my time to invest;
- you are lazy, unmotivated, or incapable;
- you are a disturbance.

These beliefs create a ripple effect, a self-fulfilling prophecy which directly influences a student's behaviour, self-worth and ability to succeed. In a 1968 Rosenthal and Jacobson study, teachers were told that a select few students had the potential for significant intellectual growth over the year. Despite these students having no difference in abilities over their peers, they showed greater academic progress in the year based on the higher expectations their teacher had of them. This positive self-fulfilling prophecy is called the Pygmalion effect, and it was concluded that 'when we expect certain behaviours of others, we are likely to act in ways that make the expected behaviour more likely to occur' (Rosenthal and Babad, 1985, p. 36). While the Pygmalion effect and high expectations can lead to positive outcomes for students, the opposite Golem effect is also true. With the Golem effect, 'students expect less of themselves, develop a lower level of motivation, exert less effort, perform at a lower level, and achieve less' (Rowe and O'Brien, 2002, p. 615). If we perceive that a student is incapable or expected to fail, they get caught in a vicious cycle that continues to perpetuate these behaviours and beliefs.

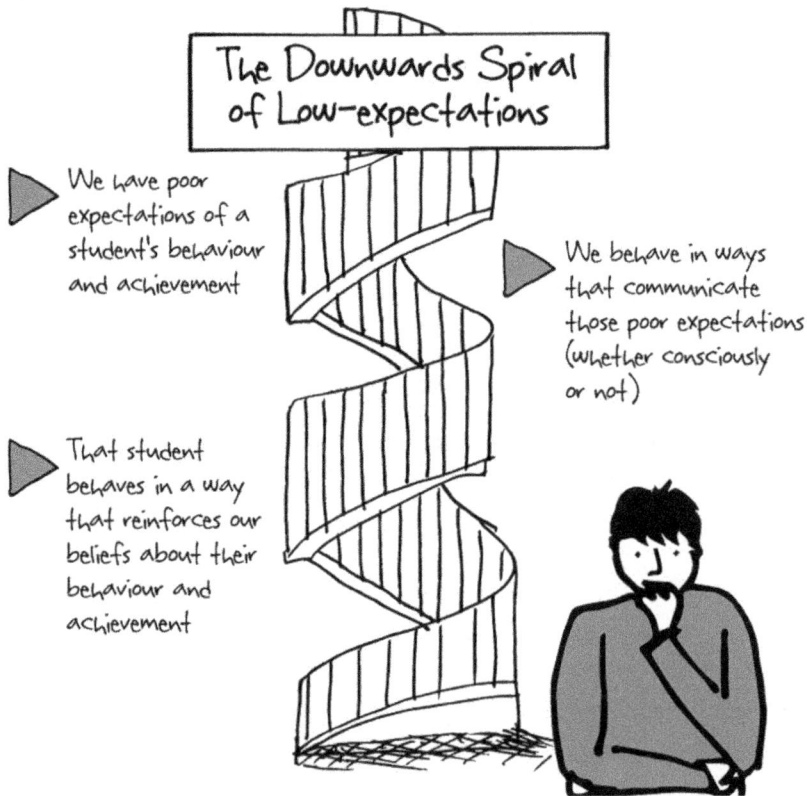

Image 6.1   The downward spiral of low expectations

As perfectly summarised by the below excerpt, when we think about our students differently, we open the door for immense positive impact and change:

Underestimating students' abilities and desires to learn a high-challenge curriculum hurts them. When students enter classrooms with skills and life experiences different from those that teachers expect, many educators mistakenly conclude students cannot – or don't want to – do complex work. When students fall short because they don't understand teachers' vocabulary or the schools' unwritten rules, teachers conclude that they lack motivation. When teachers allow pupils to sit silently during lessons or praise them for earning high grades by performing at a level that requires neither risk, stretch, nor struggle – educators underrate them. It would be better for every child if teachers thought of student potential like an iceberg – most of it hidden from view – and act upon the belief that high trust, high expectations, and high supports will reveal what lies beneath.

(Kaplan and Owings, 2013, p. 137)

Breaking the cycle

When students are accustomed to coming into a classroom where the bar is at a nice, safe and cushy low, what do you think might happen when you attempt to inject a bit of challenge? It is possible that they will respond brilliantly! It is also possible, however, that the students who are the hardest to reach and teach might meet us with a backlash of epic behaviour proportions. Others might be so deep in the cycle due to historic failure or chronic disengagement that the whole lesson is a threat before they even look at the work you have prepared.

What definitely won't do us, or our students, any good, is addressing those behaviours as an isolated occurrence – giving sanctions, suddenly pushing work completion, or keeping them back at lunch for not meeting the new goals we are setting. Hello increased survival mode! In order to raise the bar, raise expectations, increase the challenge and, ultimately, help them to succeed, we need to break that cycle. How? By shifting our beliefs and creating an environment that fosters felt safety and resilience.

Shifting our beliefs

I could have started this chapter by telling you about a multitude of students I have worked with over my career who have been caught up in the downward spiral of low expectations. It would have been easier for me and required far less vulnerability. However, their stories aren't my stories to tell. I would be assuming their feelings; I would be recounting my perception of their pain and helplessness. I didn't live it.

I wanted to tell you my story, so I can start to challenge the beliefs that we hold about our students. Through my own experiences, I can unequivocally say …

I cared deeply about my learning. No matter how many apathetic days I spent with my head on my desk, ignoring my teachers' instructions.

I desperately wanted to achieve. Regardless of how many times I came late to class or didn't show up at all.

I was capable of far more. Even with close to zero academic output in lessons.

I was yearning for connection. Despite being challenging and provocative towards my teachers.

As I discussed in Pillar 3, Be Compassionate, it is so easy for us to look at the challenging behaviours of our students and internalise beliefs about them. Being able to flip how we think about our students is how we begin to raise the bar for those who have been perpetually set one so low they can walk straight over it. This is what we can control, and this is what starts to break the cycle. However, this is no easy task, particularly with the students who are your toughest crowd. So, before I go into the *how* of raising the bar, here are some crucial reframes.

- Just because a student *appears* to not care about their learning, it doesn't mean they *don't* care. No student is waking up in the morning, *excited* to go into their lessons where they *feel like a failure*.
- The behaviours that you see are your students trying to *stay safe* in a world that might *not feel very safe*.

It is easy to forget these things when you are in the thick of it, when a student hasn't picked up a pen all year, when, despite your best efforts, they are still pushing your work off the desk or ripping it in half. However, when we continue to treat a student like they can't achieve, they will likely not achieve. This is so perfectly summed up by Daniel J. Siegel in *Brainstorm: The Power and Purpose of the Teenage Brain* (2014).

Adolescents who are absorbing negative messages about who they are and what is expected of them may sink to that level instead of realising their true potential. As Johann Wolfgang von Goethe wrote, 'Treat people as if they were what they ought to be, and you help them become what they are capable of being.'

Simply put, change starts with us and what we believe about our students.

Increasing felt safety

When was the last time you took a risk and did something new? It can be scary. Then, it becomes easy, and we no longer connect that 'thing' with the fear that we once felt.

This is why we can overlook how challenging it is for some students to trust that they are safe in our classrooms and simply 'do the work'. For some, even the act of picking up a pen takes a hell of a lot of courage, vulnerability and bravery. They are taking a risk, doing something that challenges them, publicly putting the work into something that there is a possibility of falling short on.

We need to create an environment where students feel safe to take these risks. Yet felt safety isn't just one thing. In every pillar thus far, and the pillar to follow, you will find a multitude of strategies to directly and indirectly do just that.

Relationships are a clear front runner when talking about increasing felt safety; in fact, there is a common phrase, 'Maslow before Bloom', which refers to teachers not being able to teach and reach their students before establishing a significant relationship. However, this ignores the very crucial fact that Bloom *is* Maslow in action. Establishing relationships is not just about getting to know a student's pet name or favourite movie, the way that we deliver the curriculum is another way to say: 'I care about you, you are safe here.'

Once students know they are safe, that you care about their learning, that they can take risks, that you believe in them, that they trust that you are going to give them work that they can achieve, then the reliance on the pedagogy of poverty decreases, paving the way for true learning (and, of course, fewer of those challenging behaviours).

Increasing resilience

Fiercely believing in a student doesn't mean they will get an automatic injection of success; cycle-breaking takes a lot of resilience and work on their behalf. We are able to help this along by fostering an environment of perseverance and growth mindset. James Nottingham's concept of *The Learning Pit* (n.d.) represents the journey of learning, growth and development, and normalises the feelings of fear, confusion, frustration and unknowing. By explicitly teaching and embedding this analogy with our students, resilience becomes a tangible and active part of the values and culture of a classroom.

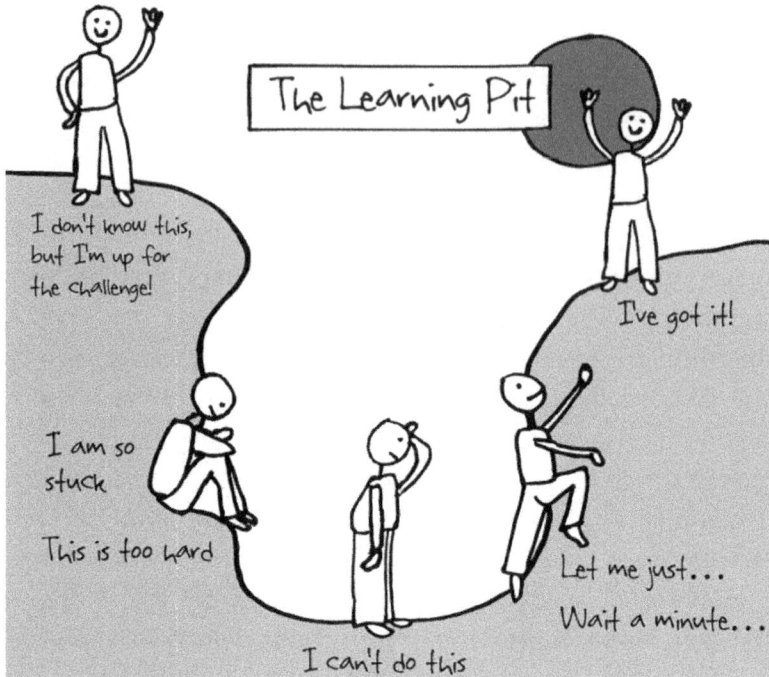

Image 6.2   The Learning Pit

An adaptation of James Nottingham's concept The Learning Pit.

How I explain the learning pit to my students at the start of the year

Imagine you are walking along and, all of a sudden, right there in front of you is a giant pit in the ground. So big that there is absolutely no way to jump over it. The side of the pit you are stuck on represents all of the things that you know and feel confident with. And as you look across the pit to the other side you can see something new. It could be a new skill like getting the basketball in the hoop, or writing an essay, or being able to do long division. But in order to get to the other side and get to that skill, you have no choice but to jump in that pit.

When you get in that pit, expect it to be a really confusing place. You are doing and seeing things you have never seen before; it can feel really difficult and scary. You will make mistakes, you will get things wrong, you will struggle. This is all necessary and normal; without this, you can't reach the other side to where you need to be. When you're in the pit, you are in the process of learning and, as uncomfortable as this is, this is actually where amazing things happen!

But you don't get out of the pit by sitting there and saying, 'This is too hard', by giving up, by cheating. If you want to get out, you have to climb out. You do this by asking questions, getting support, doing the work, practising and practising some more. Then, suddenly, you will find yourself standing over on the other side, so proud, knowing you have mastered something new, learnt something new and that is something nobody can ever take from you.

So, when you are in the pit in my lesson, when you are having these feelings, stop and remind yourself that you are about to do something new, something amazing. If you are never in the pit you are never going to grow. The more you get down in the pit, the better you'll get at climbing out of it. And nobody can do this but you.

Raising the bar

What really moves the needle when it comes to student achievement and learning? According to the extensive evidence-based research in John Hattie (2008), the leading effects on student achievement are:

1. what teachers get their students to *do*, rather than what the teacher themselves, does;
2. the expectations teachers have of their students' achievements.

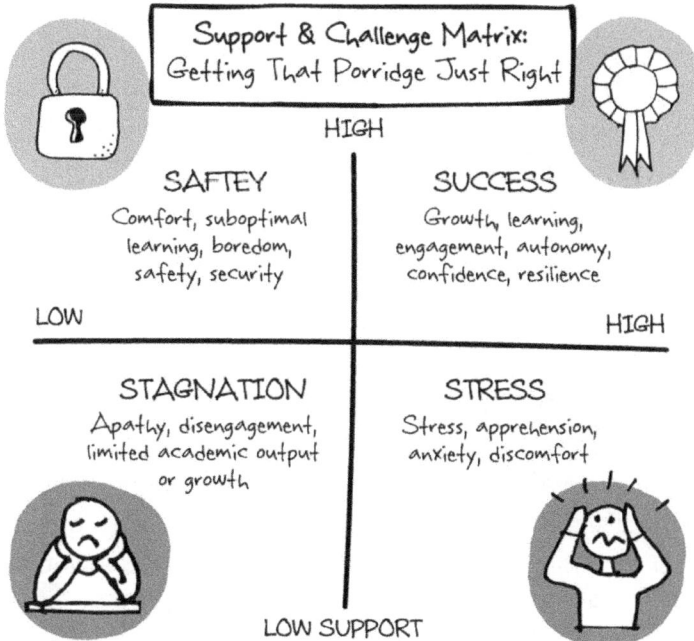

Image 6.3   Support and challenge matrix

An adaptation of Ian Day and John Blakey's Support and Challenge Matrix, first developed by and shared in their book Challenging Coaching (2012).

This means that, in order to raise that bar, we *must* be setting up an environment for our students where they can be active participants in the learning process, and be empowered in knowing that they can achieve.

The toolbox I am about to give to you does both of these things.

This is not an easy transition for students; however, when we shift away from our limiting beliefs and the pedagogies that reinforce these, towards those that foster progress and support, students begin to receive the message loud and clear: 'Not only are you *able* to do this, but I *expect* you to do this.'

Raising the bar and believing in our students fiercely doesn't mean giving them a complex task, telling them to crack on with it and letting them flail and fail. This will just compound their own negative self-beliefs and exacerbate and escalate challenging behaviours. Miss Povey knew I could do it; she knew I had the ability, she knew I wouldn't fail. Just like a teachery version of Goldilocks and the three bears, our challenge and support needs to be just right. Blakey and Day's *Support and Challenge Matrix* helps us to understand just how important striking this balance is to the success of our students.

Setting that bar low means that we are hanging out in the low challenge quadrants where safety (the pedagogy of poverty kind, not the good kind) and stagnation reign supreme. Raising that bar into high challenge means that we can have great success with our students, or, we could welcome an onslaught of challenging behaviours by increasing stress, apprehension, anxiety and discomfort. Striking that balance and pitching work in the high support/high-challenge quadrant is the ultimate teaching and learning goal; it says to students 'You can do this, and I will help you to get there.' This importance of providing the right level of support to match the level of challenge is also highlighted in Vygotsky's theoretical framework of the *Zone of Proximal Development* (ZPD). This theory demonstrates that learning is most effective when what we are working on with our students sits within that Goldilocks 'perfect porridge' of not too easy, not too hard. The ZPD can be broken down into three distinct levels.

1. *Level of actual development:* what a student can do on their own (the skills/abilities/knowledge).
2. *Zone of proximal development:* the things that a student can't do independently but can accomplish with the right level of support. It is the space between the level of actual development and the level of potential development.
3. *Level of potential development:* what the student can accomplish with the right level of support, whether it be with the help of a teacher or peer, or the appropriate scaffolding.

But how to make the porridge just right when it needs to be made at 30 different temperatures, some sweeter, some milkier, some lactose- and gluten-free, some with a dollop of honey, others with stewed apples and some loving it as plain as can be.

It is all in the differentiation, which luckily is *not* about presenting *different* work for 30 different learners.

Making that porridge 'just right'

Your differentiation toolbox

The idea of differentiation used to petrify me. I believed that it meant planning 30 different tasks, approaches and assignments. Thankfully, this is not the case. Instead, true differentiation is all about access. The following toolbox will help you hit that sweet spot with all of your students by scaffolding the learning – similar to scaffolding on a building site.

- *It's a standalone structure.* When learning scaffolds are in place and working effectively, we make students independent and autonomous. As the teacher, we don't have the strength or capacity to physically give every student a leg up in the lesson or to carry them on our backs. That's where ladders, supports and harnesses come in handy!
- *Without it, achieving the task would be out of their grasp.* A learning scaffold should *provide just enough* support for students to tackle challenges and build confidence as they work towards more independent learning and mastery.
- *It is temporary.* When the build is complete, when you know the roof won't cave in, the job is done and the scaffolding is packed away. When the time is right, when they have reached the other side of the learning pit, we can withdraw the scaffolded support.
- Although the following toolbox can't account for every single context where academic support is required, these wrap the learning up in a package of felt safety and provide students with quicker pathways up and out of the learning pit.
- Want to know the best part? You can do this without hours of additional planning every single lesson (that is what we all want to hear, right?).

Modelling: The foundational scaffold

The golden rule of *What we expect we must teach* certainly extends to what we want students to do academically. If we want to raise that bar, students need to know where that bar is, what it looks like and what it takes to reach it. This all starts with this foundational pedagogy: modelling.

I call it the foundational scaffold because you can have a lesson prepared that ticks every single 'best practice' box, yet without the modelling it could still fall short of the mark.

When we model, we:

- provide an accurate snapshot of a finished product;
- give students explicit instruction on how to utilise tools;
- demonstrate 'how to do it', whether it be a process, task or skill;
- show students what success looks like before they go off and try something themselves;
- boost confidence, reduce uncertainty and set high expectations for achievement.

All of which is the PERFECT recipe for raising the bar and providing the clarity and support needed to increase felt safety.

How to

Explain the task

Clearly explain the learning objectives and what you will be modelling. Students buy in more when they are able to connect the *what* of the lesson, to the *why* of the objective.

Do a walkthrough

Demonstrate step by step how to approach the task. This should be the best and most accurate representation of what students are about to do – for example, project the tool onto the board as you fill it out, write down the steps onto the board as you are talking through them, draw a diagram, do a physical demonstration.

Talk through your thought process and invite questions along the way so you are able to bust any misconceptions.

What it sounds like

'Once you have filled in this first box here with the technique you have found in the poem, you then go on to the example box and write down the exact quote from the text.'

Joint construction

Work together with your students to create a shared completed model. The goal is for you to step back and be a scribe or facilitator of what your students are contributing.

This process will support students to consolidate and hardwire their understanding. It provides them with a risk-free opportunity to engage with the task, see it in action one more time and receive real-time feedback before going off and doing it independently.

What it sounds like

'Wonderful! Now that you have found a technique from the poem, what is the next step to completing this table?'

Students give it a go

Students should then have the opportunity to try the task independently. Particularly if they are doing something for the first time, have the models available for them to refer to and be ready and available for questions and support.

Example of modelling

- You create a thought organiser to help students analyse a text. You project it onto the board and model completing it. You then rub it off and do a joint construction with students, acting as a scribe as they take the lead completing the tool.
- You give students a history assignment and, with it, you attach a copy of three annotated quality models of what a finished product should look like.
- You conduct a step-by-step demonstration of how to approach a new maths problem. Once you are done, you write further questions up on the board and have students help you solve them.
- You are teaching students how to bake a cake and step through a demonstration of skills as they are working through the recipe themselves.

Cheat sheets

Cheat sheets are a simple tool that, when used right, can be a powerful academic harness for students. They take away potential barriers, reduce the stress response and mental load, and help students to focus on what really matters. As students will be able to access important information quickly and easily, it will boost their independence and confidence, freeing you from answering the same questions throughout the lesson. Like an extra teaching assistant in the room!

Don't make too many cheat sheets that are 'one and done'. The last thing I want is for you to create three extra resources per lesson. A cheat sheet should be something that you could be using within your subject area in multiple different contexts.

How to

Consider what students need to know

- What prior knowledge is required to access the task/lesson (information, formulas, concepts)?
- What are the potential barriers for students?
- What questions do I foresee being asked during the task? What information can I have readily available for students to increase their independence with this task?

Create it

The cheat sheet should be developed in a way that is clear, concise and very student-friendly. If it is cluttered with too much or isn't presented in a way that is easy to use, then it could backfire and add more stress and confusion! When putting it together, use:

- clear formatting;
- step-by-step procedures;
- bullet points;
- visuals/graphs.

Share it, model it, use it

- Introduce the cheat sheet and explain the purpose of it.
- Model how it can be used as a tool to support and have them alongside students during the task.
- Keep them in a central location and continue to encourage students to independently use them when required.

Examples of cheat sheets

Mathematical formulas, historical timelines, language grammar rules, a list of literary techniques and their meaning, a step-by-step how-to for structuring a report, recipes, labelled photos showing different camera angles.

Thought organisers

Thought organisers are a visual framework that supports students to structure their ideas, organise information and make connections between concepts.

Not only does this strategy promote a greater level of critical thinking and understanding of complex topics, but having a familiar structure to organise their thoughts and ideas increases the clarity, and therefore safety, in the task.

How to

Determine the best tool for the job

What are you asking students to do for that lesson? Are they comparing, analysing, evaluating, comprehending, composing, or creating? What tool might be most fit for purpose to help organise their ideas and build them towards successfully completing this task? Here's a non-exhaustive list for inspiration:

- Venn diagram;
- mind map;
- flowchart;
- cause and effect chart;
- concept map;
- story map;
- paragraph organisers (Hamburger, PEEL);
- PEE charts: point, evidence, explain.

Create it

Don't feel you need to reinvent the wheel with the tool itself; however, be sure to adapt it to make it workable for them. I can't tell you the number of Venn diagrams I have seen students look blankly at, scribble three words into and push to the side. Ensure your tool is specific to your subject and task; on the tool itself, you could include (where appropriate):

- a heading;
- a simple 'how to' sentence students can look back on;
- labels for each of the sections;
- sentence starters or prompts;
- a vocabulary box in the corner.

As much as you can have on the tool as a support for the task, the more independence and autonomy your students will gain.

Share it, model it, use it

- Introduce the thought organiser and explain the purpose of it.
- Model step by step how they can use it to organise their responses.
- Keep them in a central location and continue to encourage students to independently use them when required.

Prompts

Sometimes students need a little help getting on track, staying on track, going deeper, or stretching further. This is where prompts come in!

Prompts are explicit instructions or questions. They are incredibly versatile and can be:

- used verbally in a class discussion to guide or stimulate the conversation;
- embedded into writing activities to initiate a deeper response;
- used as a one-to-one teaching tool to support engagement, progress and reflection;
- used to give students a much-needed boost of confidence – it is empowerment and lifting that bar in action;
- planned in advance or just come naturally within your day-to-day practice.

How to

Although prompts don't always need to be planned for, you can consider the following.

- What will the learning objectives be for that lesson?
- What types of questions might align with these and encourage the development of those skills/knowledge?
- What kinds of prompts will allow for more diverse thinking and creativity?
- Where might students get stuck? What prompts may get them unstuck?
- How can you encourage diverse types of thinking, ranging from knowledge-based questions to higher-order thinking (consider Bloom's Taxonomy).

Examples of different kinds of prompts

Prompts used in discussions.

- 'What do you think of what X just said?'
- 'Ooo that was an interesting point, can you give me one example?'
- 'What might the author be telling us based on what you just said?'

Prompts that are embedded into a writing scaffold.

- 'Use words from the question in your thesis statement.'
- 'Begin each body paragraph with a topic sentence introducing your main idea.'
- 'Explain how this technique and example supports your idea.'

Prompts for supporting students to get back on track during a task.

- 'What do you think the first thing you need to do is?'
- 'Read the question for me. What do you think it is asking you to do?'
- 'Let's take a look at your cheat sheet to give us an idea.'

Chunking down

Chunking down is a strategy where information or tasks are organised into more manageable and easily digestible pieces. It creates stepping stones for students towards goals they wouldn't think possible for themselves if they looked at the task in its entirety. This is how we can raise the bar for students who have been chronically stuck in the safe cocoon of low expectations. Chunking is useful because:

- it helps us as educators to reflect and avoid presenting information and tasks to students that are overly complex;
- it encourages students to focus on one thing at a time, reducing their cognitive load;
- it supports all students, but particularly students with additional needs (such as speaking, listening and communication needs) approach multi-step instructions and tasks more effectively;
- it helps to build a sense of achievement in students with each chunk they complete, promoting self-confidence, reducing stress and increasing independence.

How to

What is the task?

Have a look at the task you would like the students to engage with. What are the components or the steps of the task? Do a little brainstorm of the chunks that you could break it down into.

Chunk it

Divide the task into these smaller, logical segments that can be worked on either independently, or sequentially. Prepare the chunks clearly and concisely. Consider using things such as lists, tick boxes, visuals, or individual learning packs.

Share it, teach it, use it

- Communicate the task clearly, explaining how each chunk will work towards meeting the learning goal.
- Explicitly model the chunks and what is required to complete them successfully.
- Students work through the chunks in whatever way you have prepared them. Monitor students and their progress and celebrate as they move through them. Even just being able to tick tasks off a list releases happy hormones in the brain, fostering a big sense of achievement. The more mini-successes we can embed into our lessons, the more engaged and calm students will be.

Example of chunking: Writing an essay

I love to bamboozle my students when it comes to writing their first essay. At the start of the lesson I say, 'Today, you are going to be finishing and submitting an entire essay.' I am almost always met with shocked gasps from unsuspecting students. I get them to open their books, pull out the chunks we had done in the previous weeks and piece them together – showing them that they have, in fact, already successfully completed it.

The energy changes. There is an air of pride and confidence. Something that was once overwhelming, daunting and mentally beyond their reach becomes achievable. Something that they thought would be too challenging, is now something that they have done without stress or concern. The way they see essays changes. They reached the bar, and the bar was set high!

Examples of essay chunks

Chunk 1: Read and annotate the text – complete the PEE table scaffold to organise the main ideas and supporting details.

Chunk 2: Write a compelling thesis statement and introduction.

Chunk 3: Write body paragraphs, one at a time, each one based on a new row of point, evidence and explain from the PEE table.

Chunk 4: Write the conclusion.

Sentence starters

The dreaded blank page. No matter what you're doing, no matter how old you are, or what job you have, one of the most daunting parts of any process of composing is the part before you start – when you're looking at that blank page or blinking cursor.

This is magnified in a classroom context, particularly for students who already struggle academically. For these students, sentence starters are a lifeline. When they know they are coming into a room where they will have help getting started, their felt safety goes up and their stress response goes down (along with the likelihood of the dysregulated behaviours that are a result of them).

By providing ready-made sentence beginnings, not only are students helped over that mental hurdle of getting those first words on a page, but also the very act of choosing different sentence starters for different tasks expands their vocabulary and develops their skills in independently completing it in future.

How to

Where is the support needed?

- What tasks are you planning to embed into the lesson?
- What type of responses would you expect from them?
- How could they start those responses off?

Write the starters

- Prepare a variety of starters based on the types of tasks.
- Include a mixture of more basic sentence starters and more advanced, which differentiates this support to extend students' vocabulary and increase the complexity of their writing. Good differentiation helps everybody and should be designed to push learners of all levels into their zone of proximal development.

Share it, teach it, use it

- As you are modelling the task, present your sentence starters alongside it to demonstrate how they can be used effectively.
- Have students choose some of the sentence starters and model how to complete the work effectively based on these.
- To begin to remove the reliance on sentence starters, encourage students to paraphrase them, before writing their own over time.
- Keep them in a central location and continue to encourage students to independently use them when required.

Time-saver tip: Consider some different types of responses that are commonly used in your subject and create a bank of sentence starters for each. This way, you can either use the same one for different tasks, or easily adapt it when necessary. In English, I have banks of sentence starters for things such as creative writing in different genres, essay writing, short answer question responses, reflection responses.

Examples of sentence starters

- 'In his poem, Frost explores the idea that ...'
- 'One technique used to show this idea is ...'
- 'The first thing that I needed to do was ...'
- 'Similarly ...'
- 'I agree with the idea that X because X'
- 'In conclusion ...'
- 'Furthermore ...'

Exit slips

Exit slips are invaluable for all of the reasons you would expect from an exit slip. They are opportunities for students to be metacognitive, reflect on and consolidate their learning and provide immediate feedback to teachers. However, on top of those reasons, exit slips can be used as a way to hold that boundary and keep expectations high. Raising the bar is active, not passive. When we consistently check in with our students and hold this boundary through strategies such as an exit slip, the messages they hear are:

- 'I care about what you do in this room.'
- 'I will always be checking if you have done the best work you can do.'
- 'I expect you to do the work, and be successful.'
- 'If you are struggling, I will know and I will help.'
- 'I believe in you; I have the bar set high for you.'
- 'You can't opt out of learning in this class; you deserve better than that.'

How to

Create

A good exit slip should be short and sweet, simple, concise, quick to complete and quick to read. Choose questions or an activity that specifically targets the learning objectives.

Complete

Present the exit slips at the end of the lesson (or task) for students to complete. Just be sure to give them enough time to complete them; keeping students back to finish something when they haven't had enough time will breed animosity and fracture crucial relationships.

Review

Have a look at the exit slip responses to gain insights into student understanding and identify areas that may need further attention. This is where them being quick and easy to read comes into it; they should be something you can more or less take a glance at as you collect them to get a sense of where students are at.

Examples

Mini multiple choice or one-word answers that you can review at a glance.

- Choose the correct answer from the following: A metaphor is …
- Circle the three adjectives in the following sentence.
- What is a synonym for [keyword]____?

Questions (written or verbal)

- What are three ingredients that make up today's lesson? Write them in the mixing bowl.

- If you had to explain what X was to your family when you got home today, what might you say?

Or get students to give feedback on an exit slip through visuals or ratings that you can use and embed frequently.

- *Emoji ratings*: Give students a range of emojis showing different emotions or levels. Students circle the one that best represents how they feel about the learning and explain why.
- *Traffic light system*: Use a traffic light visual where green means 'I get it!', yellow means 'I have some questions' and red signals 'I need help'. Students place where they are and you can verbally discuss with them.

Success criteria

Back in Pillar 5, I introduced success criteria as a tool to increase felt safety through providing a higher level of clarity. As well as this, they enable you to explicitly show students where the bar is and how to get there. They are the explicit, clear and measurable benchmarks of what a student needs to do or include in order to complete a task or meet an outcome to the quality that is expected.

Head back to Pillar 5 to recap on what this looks like and how to embed this strategy.

Teaching and learning is classroom management

This chapter demonstrates how inextricable the link between teaching and learning, and behaviour, truly is. The way we approach the planning and resourcing of our lessons has the potential to mitigate, or exacerbate, the more difficult behaviours that might pop up. The next time you've had one of those lessons where you are getting resistance and push back, here are a few things to ask yourself.

Stop and ponder

Six questions to get curious: was the lesson to blame?!

1. Does the student lack the confidence to tackle the task in front of them?
2. Is there a barrier to the student accessing the learning?

3. Do the tasks I set hit the sweet spot of support and challenge?
4. Have I shown students what success looks like for this task and how to get there?
5. Do I truly believe that every single student can achieve the goals I have set in this lesson?
6. What messages was I sending to students about them and their learning this lesson?

Pillar 6 At a glance

- **If you set the bar low, that is exactly where they will go.** Our students will rise (and fall) to the expectations we set for them. This is not necessarily something we are cognisant of, but is constantly being reinforced through how we engage and challenge our students.

- **The *pedagogy of poverty* may be insidiously stealing your students' opportunities for success.** It refers to how low-order thinking and low-level expectations can increase control and compliance in the classroom. This phenomenon leads to the most vulnerable students being underserved in schools.

- **The beliefs that we have about our students create a ripple effect.** They are a self-fulfilling prophecy which directly influences a student's behaviour, self-worth and ability to succeed. This can have either a positive impact on student success (the Pygmalion effect), or a negative one (the Golem effect).

- **Increasing felt safety in the classroom reduces dysregulated behaviours.** Not being challenged is safe for students who have experienced historic failure, chronic disengagement, or struggle with regulation. This is why the pedagogy of poverty is rife, and explains how raising the bar can lead to an increase in the challenges that we may see with behaviour.

- **If we are to raise the bar while maintaining a calm classroom environment, we need to do so strategically**. We must increase felt safety, foster a class culture of growth mindset and resilience, and provide students with academic challenges paired with the appropriate amount of scaffolding and support.

Digging deeper

Listen in:

Want to learn more about the pedagogy of poverty and the Rosenthal and Babad study? Catch the following episodes of The Unteachables Podcast:

(Continued)

Episode 22: *Why Your Students Might Be Rewarding (or Punishing) You with Their Behaviour: A Discussion on the Insidious Pedagogy of Poverty*. Episode 28: *Are You Setting Your Students Up for Success, or Failure (Without Even Realising It)?*

Add to your bookshelf:

Visible Learning: A Synthesis of Over 800 Meta-Analyses Relating to Achievement, John Hattie (London: Routledge, 2008).

Teaching WalkThrus: Five-step Guides to Instructional Coaching: Visual Step-by-step Guides to Essential Teaching Techniques, Tom Sherrington and Oliver Caviglioli (Woodbridge: John Catt, 2020).

Drive: The Surprising Truth About What Motivates Us, Daniel H. Pink (Edinburgh: Cannongate, 2009).

Mindset: The New Psychology of Success, Carol S. Dweck (London: Random House, 2006).

PILLAR 7
Be Connected

Student, parent, teacher. It really doesn't matter who we are. Strip it back and we are all just human beings with the same deep evolutionary drive for connection, belonging and safety.

Introduction

'Good morning, Henry! It's so lovely to see you!'

'Sod off miss, you tosser.'

... Just build the relationship, they say.

'Hi Henry! Did you want to go for a little walk and chat? It'd be great to get to know each other better!'

'Are you mad? Why would I want to do that?'

Connection over correction, they say.

'How's your day been, Henry? I saw you playing basketball at lunch, you were killing it!'

'My day was fine until I had to come into this rubbish lesson and see you.'

Relationships over rigour, they say.

You see the problem here? We talk about the importance of connection, we speak about relationships as if they are the immediate magic bullet, ready to rip through and deflate bad behaviour before our eyes. Yet this advice fails to acknowledge that the students who have the biggest struggles, the ones most desperately in need of that connection, will by far be the hardest to connect with.

So, there are teachers, of course, who try their darndest to build bridges of connection. They smile warmly, they welcome students in with a clean slate, they try to tap into their love of sport, or animals, or gaming. They try, and they try some more, and students like Henry push back against them, an impenetrable force field of insults or apathy. When we continue to package up relationships as a 'cure all' for behaviour – without being realistic about what it truly takes – it creates a very lonely, disempowering and deflating place for teachers to sit in.

At this stage in the book, I don't need to tell you that a strong relationship is just one of a multitude of working parts. You could be the most personable teacher, the most hilarious, the coolest, the most connected to your students and still face enormous battles with classroom management. Because it's never just about the behaviour, and it's certainly never as easy as just building the relationship.

In saying that, despite its difficulty, developing that relationship is still a crucial piece of the puzzle. That's where this pillar comes in. I'll be guiding you to crack rapport-building with the toughest of nuts, while acknowledging and accounting for the immense challenges associated with something so seemingly simple and human.

The science of connection

For some students, it seems so damn easy to develop a great relationship, doesn't it? They are just there all wide-eyed and ready for whatever you're willing to put out. There's no overthinking it, it all comes naturally, you might have a bit of a laugh, then just get on with the learning.

It's often this simple because as human beings, we want to connect. We are biologically driven to connect. As we know from attachment theory, our brains are shaped by the connection and attachment we have with our parents and caregivers in infancy and childhood. As we grow up, the need for connection doesn't just fade away, in fact, 'social rejection in humans activates the same part of the brain as does physical pain, prompting speculation that "exclusion could be a death sentence" in human prehistory, so important was the group for survival' (Fishbane, 2007, p. 398).

So, if we are all just biologically driven to connect with each other, why are some students so resistant, requiring so much more intentionality and work to connect with? To explain this concept and frame what she coins as the 'big, baffling behaviours' we see with our students, Robyn Gobbel (2023a) describes the brain as having two settings. *Connection mode* (I am safe) and *protection mode* (I am not safe). Our brains are constantly scanning our external and internal world, seeing what threats are about, deciding what mode to switch into. If the 'danger centre' of the brain is in connection mode, our nervous systems, and our behaviours, are inviting connection; connection with ourselves, others and our learning. If the opposite is true and our brains are in protection mode, we will fight, flight or freeze, and behave in ways that are shut off to this connection (Gobbel, 2023a).

This has huge implications on how we establish relationships and reinforces the importance of creating a classroom environment that fosters felt safety through predictability, consistency, clarity, calm and support.

I would also like to take this opportunity to remind you that, as teachers, we could do absolutely everything by the book (and in this book), implement all the best-practice strategies, place down the strongest of foundations, yet a child's nervous system may be shaped by so much stress and pain that they are not able to receive it. Yet another reminder of how challenging, and how complex, this seemingly simple concept is to execute.

So, what *can* we do?

Let's talk about what putting our best foot forward with those all-important relationships looks like in practice. Trust needs to be established here – and being put into the 'safe' basket, the 'sincere' basket, the 'okay you have my best intentions at heart' basket takes more than a bi-weekly scheduled chit chat. However, realistically speaking, how can you do anything more than that with 30(plus) other students? We do so through the golden rule of connection.

> The small things are the big things.

One concept that is particularly helpful when thinking about how to apply this golden rule is the *emotional piggy bank*. A concept first developed by Stephen Covey (1999), the emotional piggy bank provides a framework for how we can intentionally invest in and foster positive and trusting relationships with others.

Each of us has one of these emotional piggy banks. Every single time we have a positive interaction, big or small, we are making a lovely loving deposit into that account. Yet relationships aren't all rainbows and riches; negative withdrawals are just part and parcel. An off-handed comment about the washing up, sorting ourselves out with a cuppa and not considering the other, or being too busy swiping on social media to ask, 'How was your day?'. These withdrawals and deposits are happening constantly; we just need to make sure we have enough deposits stored up to keep the relationship happy and functioning. Just like with a bank account, if we don't have the funds, we simply can't withdraw. The same goes for our relationships. If we try to withdraw from a relationship that we haven't been investing in, we are going to be left standing at that cash register feeling rather embarrassed and confused when our card declines (or our partner decides they have had enough and sleeps in the lounge).

Just like any other relationship in our lives, every single thing we do in our classrooms is either depositing or draining the funds. Connecting or disconnecting. The things that might seem meaningless and off the cuff, like telling a student to hurry up and get a pen out, or a sharp 'shh' as they are asking their friend for help on a question, could be enough to put us in overdraft if we haven't been investing.

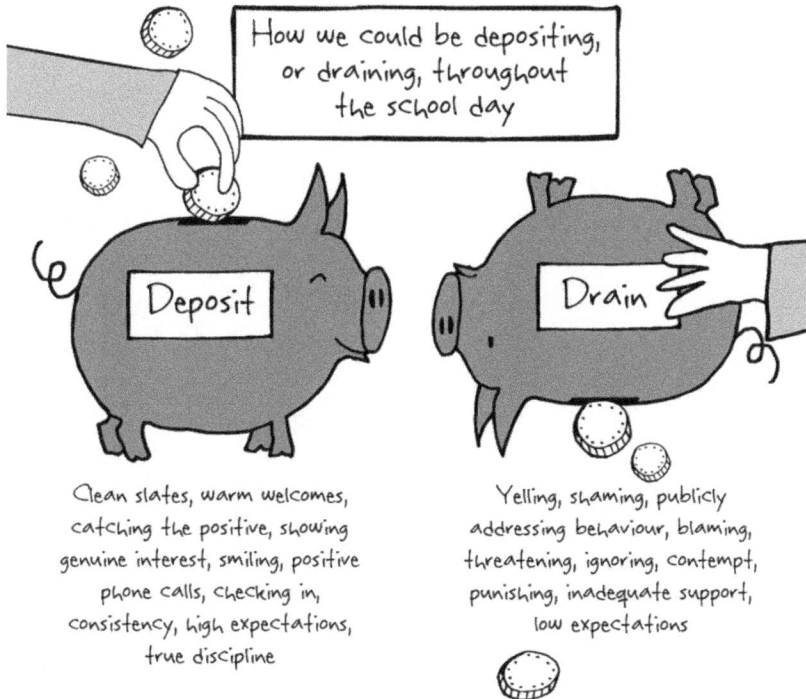

Image 7.1   The emotional piggy bank

A visual representation of Stephen Covey's concept, the emotional piggy bank, reimagined in the context of teaching.

Let's just acknowledge the glaringly obvious conundrum. The students who will require the most deposits from you to build that base of trust and rapport are likely also the ones that display the most challenging behaviours. Just as the ATM would spit out your debit card if you only had a hundred and tried to withdraw a thousand, so too will a student who you haven't invested in, but still try to address one thing after another, after another. For these students, the golden rule of little and often is crucial. Think of it as banking up a rainy-day emergency fund!

The good news is that when we address behaviours in ways that connect, respect and restore, the withdrawal becomes as smooth and amicable a transaction as possible. When we shame, isolate and punish, well that is like holding up a bank, breaking into the safe and leaving nothing but a floppy old burlap sack behind.

Investing in our student's emotional piggy bank

Pause for a moment and think about 'that' student you work with, the oppositional one, the disengaged one, the one that may have even inspired you to pick up this book searching desperately for answers. Now imagine that same student walking into classes all day long with their piggy bank in overdraft. Not a cent being intentionally deposited, but wads of cash being withdrawn.

This doesn't make it easier to work with that student, but it certainly does highlight how important, how special, how life-changing this work can be.

So, view the following toolbox not just as something that you are using to support change in a student's behaviour, but also as a way of investing in changing a young person's whole experience of education. Now, at the risk of sounding hyperbolic, when we change a young person's experience at school, there is a potential to change the trajectory of their entire lives.

Catch the positive

Our tough cookies probably don't get told many times a day that they have done something wonderful, worthwhile, skilful, or amazing. Often with these students, the positives will get clouded by the negatives and will fade into the periphery as if non-existent. This strategy is all about going out and making a point of finding them, no matter how small they seem.

When we catch the positive things about our students, we are changing the narrative and changing the game. We are shifting our beliefs and expectations, actively breaking away from the Golem effect's grasp. When we focus on the positive, we are making a commitment to seeing our students for more than their behaviours, as the human they are in the room. This is a crucial first step in moving forward and forging authentic and meaningful connections.

How to do it

Catching the positive could mean anything, no matter how big or small. The point is to show that student that you are looking past those protective barriers that they have built high around themselves. Showing that you see *them*.

- 'Gee, I didn't realise how lovely your handwriting was!'
- 'Hey Henry, don't think I didn't notice how hard you tried on that question today.'
- 'You gave things a good crack today. You should be proud.'
- 'You yelled out an answer to a question today, and I know you were doing it to have a bit of a laugh, but do you know that your answer was actually so insightful? I was really impressed!'
- 'Even just from the little bit of work you did today, I can see you've really got it!'

It also goes beyond the verbal. You can pop something positive on a sticky note, give them a thumbs up or an affirming smile, a 'great job' hi-five on their way out of the lesson. All of these things do the job of getting a student out of the negative cycle funk.

If it's not working

Take it out of the classroom and into the fresh air! You can't do this every day, with every student, but for those students you are really struggling to connect with it is an investment that could have an enormous knock-on effect.

Walking side by side with a student takes the pressure off, shifts the dynamic and makes it far easier to open up compared with a front-facing teacher/student chat.

2x10

The 2x10 strategy, originally developed by researcher Raymond Wlodkowski (1986) and popularised by Allen Mendler (2001), is a simple yet powerful intervention. Through the 2x10 method, teachers are encouraged to have short and intentional moments of connection with students. This supports the development of authentic and meaningful relationships, with a natural flow on effect of significantly decreased challenging behaviours.

How to do it

Pretty simply, as the name suggests, have a two-minute conversation with a student for ten consecutive days (you're off the hook for the weekends, of course). The success of this strategy hinges on its authenticity. This is not about behaviour, or learning, it is about getting to know them as a human being. A child will sniff you out for being disingenuous a mile away. Although it is a ten-day intervention, you can naturally keep the momentum flowing after that time!

If you're anything like me, you might be thinking about the potential awkwardness of a one-sided conversation with a resistant and disinterested student. Although I let the student drive it as much as possible and make it as natural as the situation will allow, I always have some prompts in mind, so I am not left making things far worse.

Some of my (rather cheesy) favourite conversation starters are:

- If you could pick your dream meal, all three courses with a drink, what would it be?
- If you had a teleportation machine, where would you go and what would you do there?

- Would you prefer to go back in time and meet your great great great grandparents, or go forward in time and meet your great great great grandchildren?
- What do you think is more important, being healthy or being rich? Why?
- If you could find out what would happen in the future, would you want to know? Why?
- If you won the lottery tomorrow, what is the first thing you would do with the money?

If it's not working

If you are receiving a lot of negative blowback from the student, don't push it. Instead, try to have some positive conversations with those in their friendship group and develop rapport that way. It's like getting a positive review from a trusted source. You can then offer up natural pathways into the conversation with that student in a group setting when the opportunity arises.

Positive phone calls home

For some students, their home phone ringing with school on the other end of the line could mean only one thing. Imagine if instead of the expected 'bad kid, bad news', their parent or carer put down the phone gleaming with a smile, relaying the news that their teacher had recognised them for more than the challenge. That they were celebrated for something positive. Well, that is a golden investment right there.

Not only can a positive phone call home be a huge boost for the emotional piggy bank fund, but also it paves the way for crucial dialogue and collaboration with parents and carers. When we actively recognise the strengths alongside the struggles of their children, parents and carers are far more likely to work alongside us as a team (more on navigating complex parent/carer relationships next).

How to do it

Let it flow naturally, of course! However, the following is an example of what I include to make sure it is as effective as possible.

- *Introduce yourself and state the reason for the call:*

   'Hi Mrs McPherson, I am Claire, Carly's English teacher. Are you free for a quick chat? We have both spoken a lot about some challenges that Carly has had this year, but today I wanted to touch base about some of the really positive things that I am noticing.'

- *Detail the positives and give some context:*

  'In English we have been working on some narrative writing and I have really noticed just how creative and insightful she is. She hasn't put lots of these ideas down on paper yet, I think she is just struggling with feeling confident, but what I have heard from her in class discussions and from what she has completed, I am just so happy with and want to see more of it!'

- *Ask them to let the student know you have made contact:*

  'I think Carly would really love to hear that I spoke with you today; I think it would give her a little boost. Could you please let her know that her English teacher called and fed back how she was going?'

- *Open up the lines of communication for future:*

  'Do you have any questions for me? I am always available if you do; feel free to call me or email me.'

As you can probably see, the investment toolbox doesn't have any bells and whistles. It doesn't require games or bribing with chocolate and other treats. It is simple. Small points of meaningful connection, repeated frequently enough to send the message, 'You are here, I want you here, and you matter.'

Stop and ponder

Five reflective questions to audit your emotional piggy bank investments.

1. What are the things I did today to establish the relationship, and the things that may have fractured the relationship?
2. If I were to make a list of the withdrawals and deposits I have made with that particular student lately which list would be longer?
3. What do I know about that child as a human, not just as a student?
4. When was the last time I spoke to that student about something other than their behaviour?
5. If I had to choose one positive thing right now to say to that student, what would it be?

Connecting with parents

Collaborating with parents and carers is something that tops the list of things that are pretty important. Unfortunately, when I ask, 'What are your biggest challenges in teaching?', it tops that list too. You get into the profession, ready and excited to watch your students grow and develop. Then you realise that part of this job is working with their parents/carers, a relationship that can be a complex one to navigate.

You may come across some that you call and who spout 'My child would never …'; some who jump to conclusions after hearing their cherub's very loosely put together versions of events; some that will be fuming over test results, looking to point the finger; others who expect more than you could possibly provide for their child and the 29 others in the room; some who you call about concerns and either get no answer, or a lacklustre, 'Yep, okay, bye'. All very challenging and frustrating things.

But why are these interactions so challenging? Well, it could be a variety of things.

It could just be that they are advocating for their child in the best way they know how. We need to always keep in mind that the person we are speaking to is the child's parent, carer or guardian. No matter how much we care about that student's progress and happiness, we need to start with the assumption that the parent/carer cares more about their child than we do.

For more difficult interactions, that parent/carer may bring their own negative experiences of education. As the teacher, we may represent something more for them. When we talk about being in connection or protection mode, the sheer fact that we are that figure may lead them to disconnecting and protecting through resistant or challenging behaviours.

Whatever the reason, that child succeeding is likely in the centre of both of our quality worlds. Our perceived worlds might just look a little different. Luckily for us, it is not our job to diagnose exactly what is lurking beneath, but, instead, to foster and maintain these professional and productive relationships for our students. It is just through an awareness of why these interactions may be challenging that we can stay regulated and lead them with compassion and curiosity.

How we can foster positive relationships with all parents and carers (even those that are more resistant)

A reframe

Very recently my six-month-old daughter came home from nursery with strokes of pen over her upper thigh. I felt sick, saw red, had visions of her unsupervised, laying there hopelessly as older children treated her like a piece of paper. I had a physiological and emotional reaction so strong that I had to deploy every self-regulation strategy at my disposal to not kick down the doors screaming. Of course, after calmly seeking further information, I discovered that it was simply an unfortunate incident with a dangling pen lanyard.

What this experience reminded me of was the sheer depth of emotion involved when we are working with a parent or carer. We are looking after their precious babies, and when they call with concerns, or we raise them, they need to be met on the other end by somebody who will listen. I am yet to meet a parent or carer who doesn't calm down once they feel heard, validated and reassured that we have their child's best interests at heart. With this in mind, always approach your conversations with parents/carers from a place of calm, connection, understanding and compassion.

All of the strategies that I spoke about back in Pillar 2 are just as relevant when it comes to working with parents/carers. If you are about to have a potentially challenging discussion with a parent or carer, do the following:

- Regulate and prepare for the conversation by pausing, taking a breath and checking in with yourself.
- Remember the golden rule: be what you want to see. If you want to have a calm, productive and positive discussion with a parent or carer, model that for them. Be the conductor of that energy.
- If you are feeling too dysregulated yourself and aren't in connection mode, put off the conversation until you are back to a calm and regulated state.
- If you are trying all of the above and the parent or carer is still dysregulated and things are escalating, be sure to get support from a colleague.

Getting off on the right foot

Make contact before any of the 'I need to talk to you about your child' type of calls become a necessity. The purpose of the call is to just introduce yourself and open up the lines for future communication, giving you a head start on building that crucial positive connection.

It is a five-minute investment that could make all the different to how that parent/carer responds to future discussions. Of course, it is not realistic to make 200 calls at the start of the year. Instead, create a call schedule where you can prioritise contacting the parents/carers you might need to collaborate with more frequently. Make one or two calls a day until you make it through your 'must call' list.

For the rest of the parents/carers? You can always put a letter together opening those same lines of communication.

A connected class

Oh, what a dream it would be to have a class full of students who show up willing, ready and excited to collaborate, contribute and share. Well, to bring yourself closer to this reality, it's not just about the relationships that *you* foster with your students, but the relationships, culture and community that you establish *among* your students.

Remember the analogy of the conductor and the orchestra? Having everybody playing in time (and in tune) to make a great piece of music requires a little more than breaking the ice at the start of the year. If we want to truly foster a culture of connection and collaboration, we need to be constantly taking the temperature, and intentionally warming things up when they are a little on the frosty side.

How we do this looks different depending on your context

If you're a primary teacher, you see the same team all day, every day. Although that brings with it its own challenges, you are able to embed consistent opportunities for developing that culture, the things that take a little of the day and have a lot of impact such as class meetings or conferences, daily check-ins and student roles.

For a secondary teacher, it is a little less cut and dried. How do you invest in establishing a positive 'team' culture when you have hundreds of students that you see a few times a week (if you're lucky)? Again, it's all about creating opportunities for micro-moments of connection.

A few ice-breakers

Yes, it takes more than an ice-breaker to foster that community, but of course having a strong start and getting ahead on those connections doesn't go astray. Here are three that I use for even the most resistant secondary students:

Create a class playlist: Have each student contribute one (school appropriate) song to go onto a class playlist that you can then use whenever the mood strikes. You can get them to write it on a sticky note and pop it in a box, or go around and discuss why they chose that song.

Never have I ever: Do a school-safe version of never have I ever, where students need to pop their hands in the air to fess up as you read out a list of funny school-related things. For example, never have I ever thrown my sandwich in the bin and got canteen food, pretended I needed to go to the toilet to have some time out of class, completed a whole assignment the night before. You will start to see those personalities shining through!

A whole-class handshake: Collaborate on a whole-class secret handshake that you could use every time your students enter or leave the room. Don't take yourself so seriously and really play up the dork factor! This handshake just says, 'You belong here'.

Investing in your classroom community

Investing just three to five minutes at the end of each lesson intentionally building community can have an extremely positive impact on the climate of the classroom. It can:

- inject a little novelty and enjoyment into the space;
- create opportunities for students to naturally connect in positive and productive ways;
- encourage collaboration, connection and discussion.

You *can* make these subject-specific to reinforce learning; however, don't underestimate the profound impact of spending three minutes simply having a good old chat or laugh. When it comes to the business end of the lesson, the impact of this increased enjoyment and connection can translate into having more engagement and productivity across the board.

Take the following examples, choose what suits you and your students and make them your own.

1. *Your class playlist*: If you did the class playlist ice-breaker, choose a different student's song each week to signal packing up at the end of the lesson (or wherever else you choose to use it).
2. *Guess who*: At the start of the year, request a baby photo from each student. Every week have one picture up on the board for students to guess which of their peers it is, and reveal the answer at the end of the week.
3. *Shout-out wall*: Nominate one student each lesson to write a shout-out to a member of the class (get them to write one for somebody who hasn't yet been chosen). The shout-out should recognise something positive about them or what they have done.

(Continued)

4. *A class tale*: Every lesson/week a different student adds a sentence onto a class story that sits up on a wall. You can watch it develop all of its ridiculous twists and turns over the term/year.
5. *Daily doodle*: Begin a drawing on the board and let a student add a small detail each day. Watch the drawing evolve over the term in hilarious ways.
6. *Would you rather*: Pose a humorous and out there 'would you rather' question that you then vote on and debate in the final five minutes of the lesson each week.

As Rita Pierson (2013) stated, 'kids don't learn off people they don't like'. Although I think there is more nuance to it than this quote suggests, it does highlight how crucial connections are in teaching, and reaching, every student. Ultimately, our job as a teacher is to, well, teach, and if we are to do this effectively, we need to ensure we create a classroom climate that places felt safety in the foreground, where students are open to connect with us, each other and, ultimately, their learning.

Yet, as this pillar has highlighted, the act of establishing these relationships can be a much bigger hill to climb than it is made out to be. It is through making a commitment to micro-moments of genuine connection every day that we are able to show our students that they are more than just receivers of knowledge – that they are humans in a room, and it is in that room that they belong.

Pillar 7 At a glance

- **Connections and classroom management go hand in hand.** The relationships we have with our students are a crucial piece of the puzzle when it comes to their success. However, this is far easier said than done when it comes to working with the students with the most complex needs and behaviours.
- **Establishing felt safety is crucial in knocking down barriers.** In order to overcome the challenges that we face in establishing these connections with students, we need to create a predictable, consistent, calm and supportive environment where they feel safe enough to be in 'connection' mode, rather than 'protection' mode.
- **Small points of connection every day add up to something magical.** We can begin to establish trust with students who are the hardest nuts to crack by following the golden rule: the small things are the big things.

- **Invest in your student's emotional piggy bank.** You can do this by catching the positive, having short, consistent and authentic conversations, and making positive calls home to their parents and carers.
- **Navigating relationships with parents and carers can be complex and challenging.** However, it is a crucial part of our work that we need to be well equipped to manage. By being calm and approaching each conversation with compassion and curiosity, you will be able to lead them with more confidence.
- **If we want a classroom culture where students collaborate, contribute and share, we need to establish positive relationships *among* our students.** This takes more than just a few ice-breakers at the start of the year. We need to be consistently creating opportunities for authentic connections which foster a sense of belonging and community.

Digging deeper

Listen in:

Hear me and Robyn Gobbel discuss connection and protection mode in more detail in Episode 32 of The Unteachables Podcast: *Teaching Kids with 'Big Baffling Behaviours': The Science of Opposition with Robyn Gobbel*.

Add to your bookshelf:

Raising Kids with Big, Baffling Behaviors: Brain–Body–Sensory Strategies That Really Work, Robyn Gobbel (London: Jessica Kingsley, 2023a).

The Power of Showing Up: How Parental Presence Shapes Who Our Kids Become and How Their Brains Get Wired, Daniel J. Siegel and Tina Payne Bryson (London: Scribe, 2020).

What Happened to You?: Conversations on Trauma, Resilience, and Healing, Oprah Winfrey and Bruce Perry (Monument, CO: Bluebird, 2021).

Conclusion

Although I feel the tides turning, deep in the marrow of the education system still lies an approach to student behaviour that is reactive and punitive. As Maya Angelou famously said, when we *know* better, we *do* better; and now that you have read this book, you know that classroom management is complex and all-encompassing.

Now to *doing better*.

This part is no easy feat, and it is my hope that this book acts as a mentor and a guide as you continue your journey to transform not only your practice, but also the lives of the young people you teach.

Where to start? Give yourself permission to take imperfect action.

Have awkward one-sided conversations, sound a little robotic and scripted, feel unnatural with non-verbals, create scaffolds that flop. Take those skills and practise them, hone them and hardwire them. Treat them like a muscle that needs to be strengthened and it won't be long before they become an ingrained and effortless part of your classroom management and teaching persona.

Now, I know this is easier said than done. You will have plenty of mini-critics right in front of you ready to give you immediate and brutally honest feedback. It takes bravery to step away from what feels familiar, to relinquish the false sense of control that more punitive classroom management can give you. You may slip back, falter, or forget. All of which is human and expected. Which is why you need an anchor, and the *seven pillars* and the *golden rules* are just that. Anchors to what you need to know, and do, as you make your way through this learning journey and hit its inevitable hurdles.

If you remember just seven sentences from this book, let them be these.

Be curious:
Behaviour talks, you just need to know how to listen.

Be calm:
Be what you want to see.

Be compassionate:
Happy students are rarely disengaged and destructive students.

Be consistent:
Minimise the unknown.

Be clear:
If you expect it, you must explain it.

Be challenging:
If you set the bar low, that is exactly where they will go.

Be connected:
The small things are the big things.

Yes, these seven pillars are crucial for you to foster an environment where your students can learn, connect and thrive. However, it would be remiss of me to write a book about classroom management without addressing something that is arguably more pivotal to the success of a teacher, and their students, than any other individual thing. For teachers to be successful and thrive, they too require a culture that embodies the seven pillars.

Teachers need work environments that support them to remain regulated and calm. Where they are provided with as much consistency and predictability as possible to mitigate the immense uncertainty of the day-to-day. Where they are a part of the decision-making process, and are heard, consulted and feel safe to share. Where they feel a sense of belonging, respect and safety. Where they are seen as humans first, and teachers second. Where they know they will be met with compassion and support when they make decisions and, naturally, mistakes.

So here is one final golden rule:

Championing all students, starts by championing all teachers.

If teachers aren't provided with this level of support does this mean they can't be outstanding? No, absolutely not! It just makes it a hell of a lot harder to do the job, do it well and come out with their well-being intact. This is why *true* teacher well-being doesn't look like a few cakes in the staffroom (although that certainly helps, too).

It looks like this.

A genuine commitment to placing the needs of the teacher, the heart of the education system, in the centre of what we do.

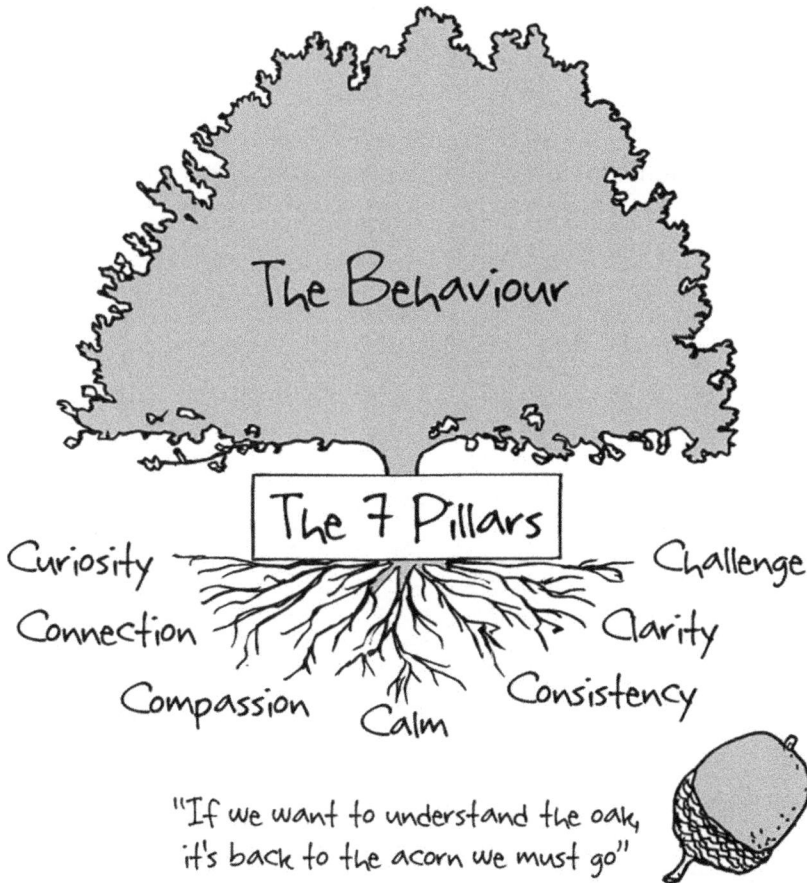

Image 8.1   To understand the oak

If we want to understand the oak, it's back to the acorn we must go.

(Winfrey and Perry, 2021, p. 22)

When you find yourself caught in the storm of challenging classroom behaviours, remember that the leaves rustling and branches swaying are far from the whole picture. Our students, us as the teachers and even the classroom climate we have fostered are all representative of the intricately linked roots below the surface. This is why we must always approach behaviour with curiosity and consider:

- what has been sown that I can't see?
- what in this lesson is anchoring them? And, finally …
- how am I showing up to weather this alongside them?

Although we can't change the roots that are already present, with the strategies in this book you are now equipped to lay down new ones, to anchor students into your island of safety, to help them grow, to help them flourish. This brings immense hope to even the most vulnerable students, and reinforces what we now know.

Classroom management is everything we are, and everything we do.

And it's certainly never just about the behaviour.

References

American Psychological Association (APA). 2008. *Are Zero Tolerance Policies Effective in the Schools? An Evidentiary Review and Recommendations.* Washington, DC: APA.

Anon. 2018. *The Facts About Teen Brain Development.* [Online] Available at: www.newportacademy.com/resources/mental-health/teen-brain-development/

Anon. 2023. *Adverse Childhood Experiences (ACEs) and Attachment.* [Online] Available at: mft.nhs.uk/rmch/services/camhs/young-people/adverse-childhood-experiences-aces-and-attachment/

Anon. n.d. s.l.:s.n. Available at: openlibrary.org/publishers/(S.l.),_(s.n.)

Arain, M., Haque, M., Johal, L., Mathur, P., Nel, W., Rais, A., Sandhu, R. and Sharma, S. 2013. Maturation of the adolescent brain. *Neuropsychiatric Disease and Treatment*, 9, 449–61.

Bellis, M. A., Hughes, K., Leckenby, N., Perkins, C. and Lowey, H. 2014. National household survey of adverse childhood experiences and their relationship with resilience to health-harming behaviors in England. *BMC Medicine*, 12(72).

Berns, G., McClure, S. M., Pagnoni, G. and Montague, P. 2001. Predictability modulates human brain response to reward. *Journal of Neuroscience: The Official Journal of the Society for Neuroscience*, 21, 2793–8.

Blakey, J. and Day, I. 2012. *Challenging Coaching: Going Beyond Traditional Coaching to Face the FACTS.* London: Nicholas Brealey.

Bradshaw, C. P., Mitchell, M. M. and Leaf, P. J. 2010. Examining the effects of schoolwide positive behavioral interventions and supports on student outcomes: Results from a randomized controlled effectiveness trial in elementary schools. *Journal of Positive Behavior Interventions*, 12(3), 133–48.

Chen, X. and Lu, L. 2022. How classroom management and instructional clarity relate to students' academic emotions in Hong Kong and England: A multi-group analysis based on the control-value theory. *Learning and Individual Differences*, 98. [Online] Available at: www.sciencedirect.com/science/article/abs/pii/S104160802200070X

Commission on Young Lives. 2022. *All Together Now. Inclusion Not Exclusion: Supporting All Young People to Succeed in School.* s.l.: s.n. [Online] Available at: thecommissiononyounglives.co.uk/wp-content/uploads/2022/04/COYL-Education-report-FINAL-APR-29-2022.pdf

Covey, S. 1999. *7 Habits of Highly Effective People.* London: Simon & Schuster.

Demie, F. 2019. The experience of Black Caribbean pupils in school exclusion in England. *Educational Review,* 73(1), 55–70.

Diamond A. 2013. Executive functions. *Annual Review of Psychology,* 64, 135–68.

Fendick, F. 1990. *The Correlation Between Teacher Clarity of Communication and Student Achievement Gain.* University of Florida. [Online] Available at: https://ufdc.ufl.edu/AA00032787/00001/images/2

Fielding, M. 2004. Transformative approaches to student voice: Theoretical underpinnings, recalcitrant realities. *British Educational Research Journal,* 295–311.

Fishbane, M., 2007. Wired to connect: Neuroscience, relationships, and therapy. *Family Process,* 46(3), 395–412.

Fox, L. 2005. *Teachers or Taunters: The Dilemma of True Discipline for Direct Care Workers with Children.* [Online] Available at: cyc-net.org/cyc-online/cycol-0205-fox.html

Gill, K. 2017. *Making the Difference: Breaking the Link Between School Exclusion and Social Exclusion.* London: IPPR.

Glasser, W. 1990. *Reality Therapy.* New York: Harper & Row.

Glasser, W. 1997. 'Choice theory' and student success. *Education Digest,* 63(3), 16–21.

Glasser, W. 1998. *Choice Theory: A New Psychology of Personal Freedom.* New York: Harper Collins.

Glasser, W. n.d. *Quickstart Guide to Choice Theory.* [Online] Available at: wglasser.com/quickstart-guide-to-choice-theory/

Gobbel, R. 2023a. *Raising Kids with Big, Baffling Behaviors: Brain–Body–Sensory Strategies That Really Work.* London: Jessica Kingsley.

Gobbel, R. 2023b. Teaching Kids with 'Big Baffling Behaviours': The Science of Opposition with Robyn Gobbel. *The Unteachables Podcast,* Buzzsprout [Podcast]. 8 August 2023. Available at: www.buzzsprout.com/2048219/13353051

Goethe, J. W. V. (1796) Wilhelm Meister's Apprenticeship. Oxford: Princeton Classics.

Grinder, M. 1995. *ENVoY: Your Personal Guide to Classroom Management.* Battle Ground, WA: Michael Grinder & Associates.

Haberman, M. 2010. The Pedagogy of Poverty versus Good Teaching. *Phi Delta Kappan,* 92(2).

Hattie, J. 2008. *Visible Learning: A Synthesis of Over 800 Meta-Analyses Relating to Achievement.* London: Routledge.

Kaplan, L. S. and Owings, W. A. 2013. *Culture Re-Boot: Reinvigorating School Culture to Improve Student Outcomes.* Thousand Oaks, CA: Corwin Press.

Klaming, R., Spadoni, A. D., Veltman, D. J. and Simmons, A. N. 2019. Expansion of hippocampal and amygdala shape in posttraumatic stress and early life stress. *NeuroImage: Clinical*, 24.

Liu, W.-Z., Zhang, W. H., Zheng, Z. H., Zou, J. X., Liu, X. X., Huang, S. H., You, W. J., He, Y., Zhang, J. Y., Wang, X. D. and Pan, B. X. 2020. Identification of a prefrontal cortex-to-amygdala pathway for chronic stress-induced anxiety. *Nature Communications*, 11(1), 2221.

McEwen, B. S. and Gianaros, P. J. 2010. Central role of the brain in stress and adaptation: Links to socioeconomic status, health, and disease. *Annals of the New York Academy of Sciences*, 1186, 190–222.

McLoud, S. 2007. Maslow's Hierarchy of Needs. *Simple Psychology*, 1(18).

Mendler, A. 2001. *Connecting with Students.* Alexandria, VA: Association for Supervision and Curriculum Development.

Nelsen, J. 1985. The three R's of logical consequences, the three R's of punishment, and the six steps for winning children over. *Individual Psychology*, 41(2).

Nottingham, J. n.d. *The Learning Pit.* [Online] Available at: cpb-eu-w2.wpmucdn.com/edublog.mgfl.net/dist/c/12/files/2016/05/learning_pit_spotlight-1d0tqab.pdf

Perera, J. 2020. *How Black Working-Class Youth are Criminalised and Excluded in the English School System.* [Online] Available at: irr.org.uk/wp-content/uploads/2020/09/How-Black-Working-Class-Youth-are-Criminalised-and-Excluded-in-the-English-School-System.pdf

Pierson, R., 2013. *TED Talks Education.* [Online] Available at: www.ted.com/talks/rita_pierson_every_kid_needs_a_champion

Rosenthal, R. and Babad, E. Y. 1985. Pygmalion in the Gymnasium. *Educational Leadership*, 43(1), 36–9.

Rosenthal, R. and Jacobson, L. 1968. *Pygmalion in the Classroom: Teacher Expectation and Student Intellectual Development.* New York: Holt, Rinehart and Winston.

Rowe, W. and O'Brien, J. 2002. The role of Golem, Pygmalion, and Galatea effects on opportunistic behavior in the classroom. *Journal of Management Education*, 26, 612–28.

Ryan, R. M. and Deci, E. L. 2000. Self-determination theory and the facilitation of intrinsic motivation, social development, and well-being. *American Psychologist*, 55(1), 68–78.

Siegel, D. 2014. *Brainstorm: The Power and Purpose of the Teenage Brain*. New York: Jeremy P. Tarcher.

Stiles, J. and Jernigan, T. L. 2010. The basics of brain development. *Neuropsychology Review*, 20(4), 327–48.

Turner, A., Belcher, L. and Pona, I. 2019. *Counting Lives: Responding to Children who are Criminally Exploited*. [Online] Available at: www.childrenssociety.org. uk/sites/default/files/2020-10/counting-lives-report.pdf

Winfrey, O. and Perry, B. 2021. *What Happened to You?: Conversations on Trauma, Resilience, and Healing*. Monument, CO: Bluebird.

Wlodkowski, R. J. 1986. *Motivation and Teaching: A Practical Guide*. Washington, DC: National Education Association.

Young Minds. n.d. *Understanding Trauma and Adversity*. [Online] Available at: https://www.youngminds.org.uk/professional/resources/understanding-trauma-and-adversity/

Index